NFT

(Non-Fungible Token)

For Beginners

THE QUICK & EASY GUIDE

Explore The Top NFT Collections Across Multiple
Protocols Like Ethereum, BSC, And Flow

MEGALODONA STREAMINGS

CONTENTS

NFT, CYBER LAW AND CRYPTO ADVANTAGES IN 8 POINTS

The first turmoil for NFTs has exploded among artists, sports clubs and gamers. Let's try to understand the usefulness of non-fungible tokens, between theoretical and practical aspects, and what precautions to adopt in their particular market.

NFT, certificate of ownership?

The adamantine tenor of object.

At first glance, the NFT can be framed as a unilateral declaration by an apparent holder with a plurilateral certification by the blockchain.

The creator of the token in the minting phase claims to be the owner of the linked underlying asset and it is this declaration that is crystallized in the cryptoblocks, which give certain date.

Cryptoblock network

Minting attributes other essential characteristics to the token, which is characterized by non-fungibility, as it cannot be replaced by goods of the same species, so is therefore unique. It is alienable because it can be exchanged, liquid because it is identified in the amount, immutable over time and in cyberspace and programmable, that is, it can be replicated according to its own coding standard.

The NFT is also an instrument equipped with intrinsic security because only the private key in the possession of the holder (initially, of the person who minted it) allows it to be used. The certainty of the object does not also extend to ascertaining the identity of who coined the token, a phase of subjective determination that goes beyond the capabilities of the NFT itself.

Therefore, we can speak of an improper certificate of ownership if we consider that in the decentralized system no authority has a priori power endowed with sovereignty and officiality on an intrinsic level, nor self-certification given the absence of an authority that provides for a notwithstanding that of certification.

NFT and underlying asset

What we have seen so far allows us to understand that the NFT does not correspond to the underlying asset. In particular, the token must be understood as the representation in the digital ecosystem of that given synthesized asset whose rights are not automatically transferred to the NFT, having to verify the correlation between the two from time to time.

Painting NFT

Nor should the circumstance that the related asset be intangible be confused. In fact, let's say that an artist's photograph is tokenized, there will always be two distinct and separate assets, the photograph (whether native .jpeg, or other format) and the NFT.

The same goes for collectible cards, called collectibles; at minting it is possible to decide how many copies of the NFT to produce. There will thus be three classes of assets: the underlying card (single), the original NFT (single) and copies of the NFT (in a predefined variable number).

If, again, the analogue work from which an NFT was minted were no longer valid, for example the securitization of a financial instrument or the destruction of a painting, the token would still not become the synthesized asset.

At the same time, the creation of an NFT does not constitute an automatic limit to the circulation of the underlying asset, be it physical or digital. In fact, once the NFT has been coined, the burden - opportunity for conservation and custody of the connected asset, be it in the form of a file subject to a certificate, even more so the physical one, because it is not loaded in the blockchain - is no less.

Difference between token and coin

The recently used term crypto is understood in the sense of cryptocurrency and not cryptography, although this latter science constitutes the pillar of the encryption standards.

A cryptocurrency coin, such as Ether, included in the Ethereum network, was started with the function of currency, a pure alternative to fiat money. As a currency, it is subject to the supervision of the competent national authorities, such as Consob in Italy, ESMA in the EU and the Security Exchange Commission in the United States, and its possession is reported in tax returns.

Ethereum coin

A cryptotoken, on the other hand, is an asset also inserted in a block network but whose characteristics, in particular its non-fungibility, leave it an identification tool for the underlying asset which, possibly, can be exchanged (NFT against asset) or sale (NFT against currency) therefore leaving its treatment very varied.

A lexical curiosity: while the computational calculation of cryptocurrencies is called extraction or mining, that of cryptotokens is called minting, perhaps a reflection of the hyper-speed of this technological sector.

THE COST LIMIT

ECONOMIC COSTS

After the first general smattering of the legal tenor of the NFT, it is essential to address its economic aspect. Use of the NFT, in fact, is not free and must be subject to weighting of costs.

First of all, it must be noted that almost the entire token world is valued and traded in cryptocurrencies.

The digital token or token gradually used have their own countervalue in current currency, but this does not overcome the current problem of the spendability of these coins and products in the real economy, probably due to the considerable volatility that still characterizes them.

Platform commissions should also be considered, that is, the top-up costs applied by websites that serve as aggregation basins for tokens and related underlying assets. And they are by no means modest.

Depending on the platform, the commissions vary from an already exorbitant 2.5%, up to as much as 15% for a first sale and 3% for subsequent ones.

The alternative to the platform is the free creation of an NFT, to be considered if you want to do without the showcase and the services offered by the platform.

A separate discussion applies to the network commissions, called gwei, which essentially guarantee the functioning of the network itself and are recognized by the miners of the cryptocurrency used.

Finally, the company costs for the qualified personnel that may be necessary for the structured use of the NFT must also be taken into account.

Environmental costs

The use of blockchain systems requires such a waste of electricity that even the United Nations has opened the discussion on the environmental impact by allocating funds for the research of eco-sustainable coding standards with low incisiveness.

The solution in the short term is, therefore, left to the market itself or, better, to the choices of individuals in the use of one or the other means considered more ecological.

In practice, however, it is plausible to extend the application of existing international regulations to crypto-instruments, for example, through the combined use of CO2 credits, and zero-impact verification systems, i.e. the so-called carbon neutral blockchains.

The Attribution Of Ownership

So far, we have observed that the NFT constitutes and acts as an (improper) certificate of objective compliance of the synthesized asset which, thanks to the blockchain system, is valid as a time stamp.

However, the verification of identity (who) and ownership (who in relation to what) goes beyond the NFT system, with the exception of one fundamental point, the name declared by the apparent owner.

Starting from this data, whenever it is required to verify the identity of the owner (seller, transferor or licensor), the contractual counterparty (buyer, transferee or licensee) or national legislation, it is necessary to ascertain who the person is who declared himself the owner and the quality declared at the time of minting. That is, both the subjective entity and the subjective attribution must be verified.

These two aspects concur on the basis of the type of goods being purchased, taking into account the uses and commercial practice. None of us, in fact, buying a television in a shop would ask the cashier for name and surname, but upon delivery of the sales tax document, we receive a lot of information, including the company name, the "name" of the selling company, the VAT identification number which, in turn, refers to the public register at the competent Chamber of Commerce where personal data, corporate purpose, significant and accounting events are collected.

If you buy a movable property, the rule of ownership is valid, so ownership is presumed in the hands of whoever physically owns the property. Therefore, if you act on your own, the ownership of the underlying asset remains presumed under two conditions, good faith and a title abstractly suitable for the transfer of ownership.

Otherwise, if you are acting on behalf of others, for example a company or a third party, the typical disciplines of the mandate with or without representation are applied, respectively in the name and on behalf of others or in their own name and on behalf of others.

Identikit

In the case of the purchase of an NFT relating to a registered movable property, the rules for the circulation of such goods still remain to be applied, by means of a public deed or an authenticated private agreement (in terms of translation and advertising effects). However, there are cases in which the dematerialization (upstream) and securitization (downstream) of the connected asset could allow its circulation, subject to the adjustment of the public registers that may mature over time.

Just consider the step-by-step role played by electronic mail and, subsequently, by certified mail. In the first case, the force in daily use has been progressively implemented and protected over time by the jurisprudence, in the second case, on the other hand, many legislative novels have intervened, to attribute a precise notification effectiveness with certification by hash imprint.

Therefore, given that the NFT is currently used for the purchase of movable property, it is assumed that the apparent owner, to whom a unique identification number is associated, is actually such. In particular, to avoid purchases from uncertain sources, it is also preferable to choose owners from platforms that contain conditions of use relating, on the one hand, to the assumption of responsibility for the declaration of ownership (or other legitimate title) during the minting phase, on the other hand, the indication of identifying elements of the owner, such as the name and surname, an identification photograph, etc.

Attention, one of the factors that distinguishes the token market is the absolute potential anonymity of those who buy and those who sell, intrinsic to the value string, where in the digital environment only the certainty of the numerical value counts and not the subject.

For this reason, we always take into account that the dissemination of personal data remains next to the chain of blocks, and is a voluntary and entirely possible act. Always considering respect for privacy, particular attention must be paid to the possession and management of personal data.

In this regard, it is enough to remember that at the beginning the first crypto-wallets were devoid of identity, following the possession of the storage device, called cold storage, while with its spread it has become common practice to provide identification data with online wallets, called hot storage.

Identity assessment tools

In the NFT panorama, we have seen that identification and subjective attribution can be compensated by auxiliary tools provided by the platforms, through specific regulatory tools.

In the future, fiduciary attribution systems could develop based on the uploading of one's own identity document, similar to what happens in the banking system, i.e. know your customer regulations. This system could broaden the audience of users, who would perceive it as a more reliable tool.

Another system, alternatively, could be double verification, which requires confirmation via token and via email or mobile phone number or even with a digital signature.

NEGOTIABILITY AND SMART CONTRACTS

After minting, an NFT can be freely exchanged. Typically, the foundation of the exchange is mutual trust.

In the legal systems of civil law, such as the Italian one, good faith and contractual correctness are required by law. Otherwise, in common law systems such as the United States, where most of the trading platforms are located, good faith and fairness must be made explicit in the contract.

Therefore, automatic execution contractual clauses can be added to the hash inserted in the block chain, with smart contracts, which are not an intrinsic part of the NFT but which govern various aspects, such as the transfer of ownership, the license, the use, copying and related prices.

The circulation rights of the NFT do not correspond to those of the underlying asset. Therefore, it is necessary to verify what you are buying, the underlying asset and / or the NFT, and it is often the platform itself that facilitates everything by indicating, for example, the license categories and the first and subsequent sale rights.

It would also be advisable to check if the owner waives the possibility of creating another NFT on a different block chain. Considering, in fact, that the various digital ecosystems still do not communicate with each other, isolation does not allow to identify a "multi-block" market, but as many as there are blockchain systems, each of which is as reliable as it is more distributed, used and capitalized.

Negotiation clauses

Among the negotiating clauses, those of greatest interest concern the transfer of economic exploitation rights.

In fact, while sales for personal and non-commercial use of the NFT are widespread, the most interesting are those smart contracts that provide for the transfer of the economic exploitation rights of the underlying work.

Looking towards the horizon, the advantage of the NFT is not only that of satisfying the need for a global and instantaneous diffusion of the asset, but also of predicting exactly which rights to transfer, which tools for reproducibility and in which territory (also the universe!) and for how long.

An NFT and an associated smart contract, in an increasingly computerized context, can lead to the correct tracking of each use and reproduction, essentially limiting what is not recovered, called Black box money.

In the future it is conceivable that, if a given work were reproduced with the NFT side by side by a device connected in the network to the various blockchains, it would be possible to define an automatic and universal tracking system from the minting to the collection of the royalty.

Global spread

The forerunner works of art

The circulation of works of art has its own practice and a special discipline on which the NFT seems to adapt almost perfectly.

In a prolific context such as that of technological innovation, the certification function of the token can take on great value.

In fact, in the trade of such works, the attribution of authenticity of a given work to a certain artist represents the first need to be satisfied. Authenticity can be attested to by the artist himself through recognition or, if no longer alive, with the adoption of expertise procedures by qualified individuals.

The second requirement consists of the attribution of provenance, that is, the verification of the lawful transfer of ownership.

The usefulness of the NFT is immediately understandable: it can act as a perpetual certification of authenticity and provenance because, by binding to the underlying work, it traces the changes of ownership up to tracing back to that of origin, or up to the first tokenized one.

The result therefore consists of the reclamation of a good part of the illicit phenomena of counterfeiting and money laundering, to guarantee the quality of the purchase and of the work itself.

Photography

The certification function can also be used in the photography sector.

Let us think, in the meantime, of artistic and simple photographs.

Bohemian storm

The minting of an NFT to which a smart contract is combined would make it possible to take advantage of both the benefit of certification and the collection of the proceeds deriving from their economic exploitation.

In fact, it is with the same smart contract that both the duration of the exploitation constraint and the territorial extension can be set.

Thus, it is possible to effectively protect simple photographs for twenty years from their production and artistic ones for seventy years after the death of the artist.

Music

Musical works can be the object of NFT through the encoding of the audio file.

Considering that both the composition rights (e.g., lyrics and melody) and those for sound recording (e.g., the Master) must be regulated, it becomes crucial to define the amount of royalties due to the minting of the NFT.

All this must be integrated with a smart contract that regulates the regime of assignment or licensing of copyrights, thus managed by the publishing houses, and those on audio recordings, by record labels.

A practical application could be given by a streaming music app which connects the musical works to an NFT, directly activating the rights connected to the token and the smart contract when used. The result would therefore be the automated distribution of royalties to the publisher, the label and the author using the information provided by the blockchain structure itself.

Such a system would essentially become a second track with respect to national databases and would guarantee the resale right, since the owner (prevailing) could graduate the first sale and second sale (and subsequent) rights.

Cinematography

Even in the field of cinematography, the complex sequence of images and sounds can be encoded in a hash registered in the blockchain.

The NFT for this type of work can be assisted by a smart contract that regulates the rights of exploitation up to seventy years after the death of the last of the individuals identified.

In all likelihood, the figure of the producer will be entitled to the NFT, governing the exploitation and collection regime, similarly to what is indicated in the music streaming sector.

STOCK EXCHANGE AND FINANCE

NFTs in finance already have their own name: De.Fi.

An acronym for distributed finance, or decentralized finance, this token encodes a financial product, such as a cryptocurrency loan.

The particular utility of De.Fi. is the solution of double spending, a phenomenon whereby the deception of a token produced by a centralized and undistributed system can be manipulated to be reproduced illegally?

The financial token therefore remains distinct and parallel to the traditional financial system, being able to constitute a widespread and verifiable space on a global scale. Furthermore, the use of De.Fi. such as tracking tools for dematerialized securities, associated assets with the related equity and voting rights.

Decentralized finance

Gaming

As seen for the loot boxes, different objects are continuously exchanged in video games.

The NFTs, here called friendly nifty, are part of this process allowing the univocal attribution of a copy of the original NFT, created by the publisher (or developer) of the game.

The initial creator defines how many copies of the NFT to make, which gamer collectors will purchase.

NFTs could usher in a revolution in this area. Going a little further, in fact, they could allow the insertion of the unique hash into the game and allow the player to use that precise object, item or skin.

It should be considered that, to date, manufacturers rarely allow the exchange of items between players, especially outside the store or the game itself. However, opening up to NFTs could represent a new source of revenue with the provision of reusable NFTs for the payment of a fee established upstream.

The protection of the NFT

The theoretical purchase and sale of NFTs on the internet would allow the reference to the typical cases of competent court and applicable law of national or international private law, taking into account the location of the parties.

However, it is noticeable that the paucity of information on the identity of the parties does not make this task easy in practice.

Since these are, by their nature, purchases on the internet, in particular on websites, the place of jurisdiction is the place where the order confirmation is received, i.e. the residence, domicile or home of the purchaser.

Open NFT

If, however, the buyer's acceptance must be sent to the seller via email, i.e. outside the website showcase, the place of jurisdiction will be that of the seller's residence, domicile or home.

Pay attention, therefore, because in the event of a contract stipulated on the platforms it is very likely the application of the first criterion, while outside of them, for example via email and IPFS, it is necessary to verify which of the two hypotheses to apply.

In the case of a sale between a professional seller and a consumer buyer, the place of jurisdiction will be that of the latter's residence, domicile or home.

As for the applicable law, it should be borne in mind that in practice the platforms, mostly American, make express reference to the legislation of the United States, in particular the Digital Millennium Copyright Act, i.e. the special legislation on copyright.

Finally, it must be considered that, in addition to the NFT, each category of underlying asset may correspond to the various disciplines and special protections such as, in fact, that relating to copyright, cultural heritage law, industrial law (relative, among the others, to trademarks, patents and industrial designs), banking law and financial market law.

NFT, tax profiles

So far we have observed that NFTs can be seen both in their function as improper certificates and as assets.

Furthermore, NFTs have their own negotiating value but do not act as a medium of exchange, therefore they are distinguished from coins by not taking the form of currency.

Again, if NFTs are stored in a widespread way, even on a global scale, it goes without saying that these assets are not peacefully located even outside national borders. In fact, the capillarity of the distribution of data on IT devices does not allow the identification of their location, therefore being able to consider the predominant character of territoriality, which in turn can be arguably compensated in tax matters by the foreign location, because fictio iuris.

To this we add that the circulation of a token originally assumes a non-commercial connotation, as a good capable of satisfying a life need, for example the use of a work of art or the viewing of a film. In other cases, to be distinguished from time to time, the sale of an NFT can take on the nature of an investment due to the prevalence of the use of capital, while the qualification of the relationship having a random nature, i.e. a speculative instrument, can be excluded.

In conclusion, the use of NFTs seems to have just begun to take baby steps. Perhaps with a gradual approach hand in hand with technological integration, some executive processes can be streamlined with this automatic tool, as long as it is made more digestible for the general public.

NFT: WHAT THEY ARE AND HOW THEY WORK
[COMPLETE GUIDE]

NFTs – an acronym for Non-Fungible Tokens - are unique tokens that represent a digital property on the blockchain. They have become very fashionable, with auctions of tokenized artworks that have surpassed the prices of the most famous painters in history.

In reality, however, there is much more to the world of NFTs. A very interesting technology that is already used by many large companies, able to create marketplaces on blockchain of everything that can be tokenized. In our in-depth analysis we will talk about the technical specifications and investment ideas that this technology offers, by separating fashion from what is the concrete basis of this new way of interpreting the blockchain.

Main features of NFTs:

- What does NFT mean: Acronym for "Non Fungible Token"
- Which are the best today: Chiliz / Theta / Decentraland / Enjin Coin
- How to invest: Trading and direct token purchase
- Best exchanges: Coinbase / Crypto.com / Binance
- Best trading platforms: eToro - Capital.com

The main introductory features to NFTs

What are NFTs?

Scholastic definitions are unlikely to be able to render, with due depth, all the aspects related to a new technology. For this reason, it will be necessary to address some of the most important issues concerning the world of non-fungible tokens before moving on to more advanced topics and also to possible practical and commercial applications.

The first thing to understand is already in the name of this technology. NFT - Non-Fungible Tokens - are opposed to fungible tokens, that is tokens that do not have a specific individuality and that can be replaced with other tokens of the same kind. The most striking example of this quality can already be seen outside the categories of the blockchain.

Money, even in the form of banknotes that we have in our wallet, is fungible by definition. If we were to give Marco $10 tomorrow and he were to give us another $10, there would be no difference in the composition of our assets. Each $10 bill represents identical value. And for this reason, money can be considered fungible.

But now let's think, for example, of a painting: it is a unique piece, there is nothing identical in the world. It can be sold for money, but it cannot be exchanged for an identical painting that has the same value. A work of art is by definition non-fungible, because it cannot be exchanged for a generic and identical good in value.

Token fungibility

NFTs represent non-fungible assets, as opposed to cryptocurrencies.

NFTs are the work of art, in our example, and classic cryptocurrencies such as Bitcoin or even Litecoin (for example) are money. If we exchange a Bitcoin for another Bitcoin, nothing will change in our balance sheets, because a BTC is always identical to a BTC. In the case of possession of an NFT token though, we will have a unique piece in our hands.

On blockchain

Just like classic crypto tokens, NFTs are also traded via blockchain. As should be known, the blockchain that currently supports them most frequently is Ethereum, which offers two different ERC standards for creating NFTs. As we will also see later, there are several projects and blockchains that allow you to create your own NFTs and exchange them.

The blockchain offers the advantages we all know for this type of exchange: they are registered, they have solid mechanisms to validate transactions and above all they are freely accessible. Which means that verifying ownership of a given token is simple.

The problem of algorithms for the validation of NFTs

The ecological theme seems to be one of the arguments most used by detractors of the world of blockchain and cryptocurrencies to attack this type of system. The same controversy has also been used to report the ecological impact that systems such as NFTs that are based on PoW blockchains would have. That is the old way - exorbitant under the electrical plan and calculations - of validating new blocks of a blockchain.

NFT pollution

Pollution is a minimal problem, which will soon become non-existent.

The fact is that with the 2.0 upgrade even the main blockchain that today supports NFTs will switch to a completely PoS system within a year, capable of consuming 1/100 of the energy while offering the same level of security. Even the ecological criticisms, in reality already very poorly founded today (a transaction of an NFT does not have such a great impact), will have to surrender in the face of the advancement of NFT technology.

Metadata

An NFT includes metadata, which accompanies an image, file, audio track, or any other type of data to the token. The data is always freely available, at least on the most popular blockchains for this type of token. There is nothing to prevent the incorporation of any type of data as a representation of the title of ownership. For example, the sale of the first Tweet by Jack Dorsey, the founder of Twitter, will go down in history. Properly transformed into an NFT.

NFT metadata

Within the metadata there can be any type of digital representation.

To represent the property

The most common use we can make of NFTs is digital property representation. Most of the systems that support NFTs today allow you to tokenize a digital work of art, be it an image, or even a song, or a video. Although a video is perfectly reproducible, as well as the image or the song, an NFT represents the property of the same.

For artists (NFT Art)

Among the first to take advantage of technology were artists, who have found a relatively simple way to support their art, with fans finally being able to finance works, which will remain usable for all, among other things. There are many artists, digital and otherwise, who have relied on this type of technology to spread their works and find financiers. Have we solved the problem of the need for patrons even for less famous artists? Absolutely not, but the prospects that NFTs offer are certainly good.

Non-Fungible-Tokens - exactly how do they work?

We have broadly understood what NFTs can be used for, but what does blockchain have to do with it and how exactly does this type of token work on a technical level? We will have to introduce some additional concepts in order to actually understand how they work.

ERC standards

Even if the Ethereum blockchain is not today the only one able to support NFTs, it is from this that we will start for an example as general as possible, to understand how NFTs work. The most important of the standards used today is ERC 721, which provides relatively simple rules for creating a single token on the Ethereum blockchain. The standard in question is the same, for example, used by projects like Decentraland, like CryptoKitties and also like CryptoBeasties.

The creation of the NFT

The token is created on the blockchain, incorporating a unique ID that represents it and with indications on the metadata it incorporates. It is at this stage that we create a unique token, which is different from all other NFTs and which is uniquely identified. The creation also assigns this token to a wallet capable of storing ERC 721 tokens, or alternatively the standard that we have decided to use.

How NFT works

The operation of NFTs is straightforward and simple.

The possible exchange

Being crypto tokens in all respects, which are in fact supported by a real blockchain, these tokens can be exchanged both through smart contracts and through manual exchange. They are in effect assets that we can buy and sell - and for this purpose, many markets have also sprung up that allow auctions or private agreements.

What does the token represent?

Ownership - although in some jurisdictions it is not yet perfectly clear how these rights will be enforced. What matters, at least for the moment, is that the blockchain can guarantee good levels of security both for the storage of NFT tokens and for the exchange. Those who have followed the world of cryptocurrencies for some time will know that these systems are among the safest to make transfers permanent. This concept, applied to the world of NFTs, exposes the enormous potential that this technology may have in the future, even in economically important markets such as that of art.

Bragging rights

NFTs certainly move the concept of ownership and possession into a whole new field. If we were to look at the auctions that have been most successful in recent times, these are transfers of ownership of digital objects that are actually available to everyone. Everyone can still read the first Tweet in history, just as anyone can technically endlessly copy Banksy's artwork that ended up at Christie's auction.

What did those who bought this type of token actually acquire? Property in the strict sense, which given that in this case it does not offer the exclusive enjoyment of the property - which remains digital and accessible to all - has been considered by some commentators as a mere right to boast of the property itself.

NFT - ownership concept

The right to brag, but that's not all. The concept of ownership can be revolutionized by NFTs

There are actually many other levels involved in using NFTs. Let's think of cases like that of Decentraland, where NFT LAND tokens allow you to have exclusive use and privileges on a virtual area of the game. In this case one of the fundamental attributes of ownership, namely the power to exclude someone, is fully preserved. The same can be said of systems, such as fan tokens, where the possession of certain NFTs offers special privileges and access to merchandising. In that case the NFT really gives the owner an exclusive right, which non-owners do not have.

To avoid the useless ruminations that we have already read in the non-specialized press, we invite everyone to focus, at least for now, on the strictly technological aspect of the story. NFTs offer a safe, fast, and inexpensive way to tokenize works of human ingenuity and to securely transfer them to others. Whether you rely on the Ethereum or Tron network, or on the many niche systems, it doesn't matter.

Just as it matters little what the present and future fields of application of this technology will be. Because it is true that fashion has created auctions with closures that are almost impossible for a reasonable mind to understand. But it is equally true that these are in fact full-blown advertising operations, which have nothing to do with the actual future of this technology.

Best 7 NFT Projects [Non–Fungible–Token Ranking]

We have selected the seven best projects that also support NFTs, with a good mix between those that are generally involved in supporting the standard and those that make it an integral part of their very raison d'être. The list you will find here is constantly updated and is to be considered valid at any time it is read.

THETA

Theta is an advanced blockchain created to offer decentralized distribution of video content, trying to overcome the concept of CDN currently used by the main streaming services worldwide.

Our Theta fact sheet

Among the co-founders of the project we find Steve Chen, founder of YouTube at the time and able to attract the attention of even very large groups, as evidenced by the participation of Sony, Google and Samsung in the project.

THETA - Table of main introductory features

With the transition to version 3.0, Theta also supports the creation of NFTs, which can be managed internally to the network, paying the fees and gas with the parallel TFUEL token. The project has been growing rapidly since the beginning of 2021 and although not focused only on NFTs, it will be able to create further enthusiasm thanks to the support offered by this technology. We can find Theta tokens from Capital.com (you can sign up for free here for the demo account), which offers the possibility to invest in various emerging cryptocurrencies through its platform.

Chiliz

The blockchain that is connected to the world of football fans and sports in general has already established very important collaborations with all the major clubs.

Name: Chiliz

Abbreviation: CHZ

Founded: 2018

Technology: Support for teams and fans

Wallet: ZenGo, Trust Wallet

A commercially strong project, which recently signed an agreement with Chainlink to start creating NFTs in real time. They will be, at least according to the projects, extremely innovative NFTs. Because thanks to the oracles of Chainlink, NFTs can be created whose value and functioning is linked to sporting events in real time. The project's reference cryptocurrency can also be traded on Capital.com (here to sign up for the free demo), a broker that has always been among the most attentive in the world of emerging cryptocurrencies and which, first in the world, has included Chiliz in its lists.

Enjin Coin

Enjin Coin is the token of one of the most complex and integrated blockchains currently available on the market. Its focus? The world of online video games and everything that revolves around it, also in terms of community.

Inside, in fact, we can find excellent infrastructure for the exchange of rare or unique items of different online games. In addition, with the Beam service, support is also offered to content creators for the expansion of their audience.

Name: Enjin Coin

Abbreviation: ENJ

Founded: 2020

Technology: Infrastructure for online game items and content creators

Wallet: Ethereum compatible

The reference token, Enjin Coin, has been the subject of one of the most incredible growths of 2021 and is used for the purpose of the platform as a free currency. An integrated project, which looks at the world of online video games and content creators and which could have its say in one of the potentially most lucrative sectors of the future of blockchains. This token can also be found on Capital.com (you can open a free trial account at this address) - treated as a common financial asset, to which we can apply technical analysis and even advanced order management.

Decentraland

Decentraland is a virtual world in Second Life style (which many of our readers no longer very young will remember) or if we want, in Minecraft style.

This project also makes extensive use of NFTs, through its LAND tokens, which represent a Smooth plot of land within this virtual universe.

Name: Decentraland

Abbreviation: LAND / MANA

Founded: 2018

Technology: Virtual world - NFT token for land acquisition

Wallet: In-game Token - for MANA: MetaMask

Decentraland uses a double currency system: on the one hand we have the MANA, which is the fungible money of the game, on the other hand we have the LAND tokens, which represent the ownership of virtual spaces on which we can create and install commercial activities, always virtual or any other type of construction suitable for the game. This is one of the typical cases of application of the NFT concept.

Each token is not fungible and incorporates the ownership of the plot and the location of the same. We can sell and buy the token, which is not the same as any of the other LAND tokens in the game. On Capital.com - you can join the platform for free here - we can invest in MANA, which is the fungible part of the tokens used in the Decentraland multiverse. A great way to proceed if we believe in the growth of this virtual world.

Flow

Flow is a blockchain infrastructure dedicated exclusively to the world of NFTs. It is the go-to platform for creating and trading the popular NBA Top Shot and has also been chosen by UFC for its next series of digital collectibles.

The reference token is the fuel of the project and must be used to pay for transactions, thus constituting a good investment should Flow, as a project, continue to grow, in a commercial sense.

Name: Flow

Initials: FLOW

Founded: 2021

Technology: Complete infrastructure for NFT

Wallet: Dapper Wallet

Flow can only interest the very important partnerships that have already been closed by the group. NBA, Samsung, Dr. Seuss, Warner Music Group. A heterogeneous group of very large companies, which testify to the firm basis of the project. Flow is currently one of the most interesting blockchains, commercially speaking, among those that can offer support to the world of non-fungible tokens. We can also find Flow in direct purchase on the popular Kraken exchange, which has long since included it in its lists.

WAX

Wax is a very interesting blockchain, because it also integrates an NFT marketplace that has already attracted the attention (and creations) of big players in the entertainment sector.

This was the blockchain that hosted the deadmau5 auctions, as well as the creation and sale of NFT by Atari and Capcom, two very important companies in the video game sector.

Name: WAX

Abbreviation: WAXP

Founded: 2018

Technology: Complete infrastructure for NFT

Wallet: Wax Cloud Wallet

The WAX blockchain is governed by WAXG tokens and rewards participants via Ethereum. It is currently one of the most developed in the sector, also offering toolkits to develop decentralized apps and to support the construction of contracts and automatic exchanges. The project is still in progress, although it has already made some very important collaborations. Interoperability with Ethereum's ERC 721 and ERC 1115 standards will also be available shortly.

MyNeopleAlice

Another virtual world project, a video game to participate in via the internet, which allows us to purchase NFTs that represent objects, real estate, clothes and any other type of item that can be created in the game. This is also a rather typical case of application for the world of NFTs, which will in all probability be adapted and replicated even by much stronger companies commercially.

The project is based on two levels: there are those who simply want to enjoy the game and can participate in yet another multi-verse which, by the authors' own admission, is made to resemble the world of Animal Farm very closely and attract collectors attracted to NFTs.

Name: MyNeopleAlice

Abbreviation: ALICE

Founded: 2021

Technology: Online Game

Wallet: MetaMask

The project is still in a relatively embryonic stage, although it already has a decent following and a good number of NFTs that have been produced. The most important NFTs represent ownership of virtual islands in the MyNeopleAlice universe.

We presented the 7 best projects that support NFT today, both for the functioning of its commercial networks, and to support marketplaces or the functioning of the services they offer. However, they are not the only ones. There are in fact many other newly born projects, which will fight to conquer, at least in part, the lucrative niche of NFTs.

IDENTIFICATION NFT TECHNOLOGY

RLC iExec RLC Business data management

OMI Ecomi Collectible digital property pop

SAND The Sandbox Minecraft-style virtual world

RFOX RedFox Labs NFT for gaming

SUPER SuperFarm Multi-chain NFT creation and management

AXS Axie Infinity Pokemon-style digital universe

TVK Terra Virtua Kolect Digital collectibles

UOS Ultra NFT for gamers

CHR Chromia Infrastructure for NFT creation

ERN Ethernity Chain NFTs authenticated by third parties

DEGO Dego Finance Infrastructure for generic and financial NFTs

GALA Gala Multiverse for online games

WHALE Whale NFT infrastructure for comics, digital art and virtual worlds

REVV Revv NFT supporting racing-based video game

DG Decentral Games Virtual casino accessible online - with associated multiverse

NFTX NFTX Creation of funds with NFT baskets

MEME Meme NFT for digital art

GHST Aavegotchi Tamagotchi-style NFT - unique and exchangeable with other users

LYXe Lukso NFT for the production chain and transparency towards customers

GET Get Protocol NFT for mass event tickets

GAME GameCredits NFT for creating items in online games

BONDLY Bondly NFT collections on different chains

DMT DMarket NFT for Esports

While they failed to make it into our special ranking of the top 7 NFT projects, many of these ecosystems already have a good commercial impact and - we are relatively certain - will start to be talked about shortly.

How can NFTs enter everyday life?

NFTs, while very popular, are still not part of everyday life for the general public. Or rather, they are slowly becoming so, also thanks to projects that already involve the world of sports, films, video game collectibles. In addition, NFTs can also be used in the future for tracking supply chains and for verifying the origins of clothing, which actually already exists in a very popular sportswear brand.

EXAMPLES OF USES OF NFTS

If it is true that NFTs are still something of a niche, it is equally true that there are already many projects that make concrete use of them. Here we will mention some of the most interesting projects that are already in full swing and that have shown, if there was still a need, that in reality the world of NFTs can also offer a lot to sectors other than art speculation.

Decentraland and video games

We have already talked about it in the section specifically dedicated to the best NFT systems currently on the market. Decentraland may be a pilot case, which could be revised and improved by more commercially structured projects. It is not certain that in the future we will not be able to see these systems applied to more popular games, such as World of Warcraft and all the other very successful MMORPGs.

NBA Top Shot

The world of stickers and fantasy basketball has already moved, at least in part, to NFTs. The NFT Top Shots project is proof of this. It runs on Flow infrastructure - which we have already talked about in this guide - and distributes digital stickers of the best NBA players for a fee. And the strongest players, like LeBron James, ended up in the auction for six-figure values.

UFC: collectibles

The hugely popular MMA circuit will also soon make its debut on the Flow network, offering digital collectibles through NFT technology. Another huge franchise that chooses the digital path of the future, recognizing the good things a system of this type can offer even to sports collectors.

Sorare: global fantasy football

Another very interesting project that today uses NFT technology is Sorare, which offers a sort of fantasy football game on a global scale, which also relies on the world of NFT. Also in this case we are faced with a decidedly futuristic project that focuses on the best possible technology for the management of multiple and even unique cards. The Cristiano Ronaldo card was sold for just over $290,000.

Nike and the CryptoKicks

One of the most popular brands in the world of sports has long been thinking about how to take advantage of the incredible fashion of NFTs. And it did so through the CryptoKicks project, tokenized shoes within the Ethereum blockchain. In the future, the system can also be used to certify the scarcity of certain collectible models and their originality.

NFT Opinions and real reviews

The explosion of NFTs has led to a flood of comments, opinions and reviews both in print and on the Internet. It is certain that with time - and with the greater diffusion of NFT technology, more channels and more information sources will be found with a correct approach to non-fungible tokens.

Authoritative opinions from famous experts

Several commentators of classical economics, if we want to call it that, have also expressed themselves on the world of NFTs. Opinions that (and this will surely leave some of our readers stunned) are on average very positive.

Bloomberg

The famous network dedicated to finance - quintessential to international capitalism - has expressed itself on several occasions on the phenomenon of NFTs. The most important comment is certainly that of Leoind Bershidsky, who in a long article explained to the readers of the website of the popular network that NFTs are here to stay and that they will become increasingly important for the world of art and collectibles. A sector that is a game for the rich regardless of the technologies involved and which therefore would not have profoundly changed its nature even with the arrival of non-fungible tokens.

Fortune

Another publishing network for those who want to know more about investments. Even this famous newspaper, which holds the famous classic Fortune 500, has dealt with NFT several times. The most important piece published by this big organ of financial information is signed by David Z. Morris, who explains to an audience perhaps more calibrated on the stock market, the revolution in the concept of ownership and art in the era of art on blockchains, i.e. in the era of NFTs.

Our take on Non-Fungible-Tokens

NFTs are the fashion of the moment, despite having been around for several years now, albeit previously in much less advanced forms. If on the one hand there is certainly fashion to push prices up, on the other hand we find concrete applications - even commercially - increasingly vast for this type of product.

The birth of many blockchains capable of supporting them - which we have adequately illustrated in the course of our guide - tells us of an embryonic situation, but one which is rapidly gaining traction within the world of blockchain and also in the markets for the exchange of property rights.

NFT technology can revolutionize the world of video games, collectibles and even decentralized finance, as it is already widely used in the management and control of supply chains and value chains. The potential is enormous, despite the fact that today it is talked about almost exclusively for the crazy-priced auctions that hit the headlines.

We are still in an extremely experimental phase of the world of NFTs and the prices of some of the assets at auction reflect this extremely immature state of technology and the markets that surround us. However, there are other considerations to make in this regard, that do not help us at all to understand the present and the future of this type of ecosystem.

Yes, they will be a very valid channel for the ownership of artistic works.

We have very few doubts about this. The auctions that have already been held at Christie's and Sotheby's will lead to a massive entry of NFT technology into the art market. We believe that there is no doubt about it: NFTs are a smart, fast, safe and cheap way to exchange ownership, digital and otherwise, of works of art.

Revolution for the world of video games

Where there were already several companies that were managing very complex economies, not having the possibility of delegating exchanges to efficient third-party systems such as the blockchains that host NFTs, we already have clear evidence that NFTs will become the standard for any kind of virtual world, present and future. And whoever fails to comply will end up losing a huge number of profits.

Where will NFT be used?

NFTs have huge future prospects.

NFTs will also be a turning point for collectors.

And even on this there is very little doubt. We are not just talking about collections of digital works, but also about physical objects. Let's imagine, for example, the trading card sector, which today sees many speculators taking part in auctions. A Pokemon or Magic the Gathering card can exceed $100,000 in value. Physically moving them is expensive and risky. When third parties emerge to guarantee the transaction, they can be kept in banks or custody services and to pass (and guarantee the passage), it will be only the NTF token that represents the ownership of the card.

For finance: OTC contracts

We enter a territory for specialists. The OTC market could find in the blockchains that support NFTs an excellent support for the transfer of customized contracts, without having to refer to internal clearing houses: expensive and unsafe and, above all, exposed to human error.

Many derivative investments with specific contracts could find an excellent ally in NFTs.

There are many sectors that NFTs will be able to revolutionize. It is not certain that they will succeed with all the sectors that are currently taking an interest in this technology. But the prospects are more than interesting and open to very positive scenarios, especially for those who are now entering the market.

Final remarks

NFTs are partly fashion, partly a very interesting technological solution, which can really make a difference in the management of digital and non-digital properties. Even for those wishing to invest in this sector, today there are two ways: focus on exclusive works of art - and therefore speculate on their possible revaluation, or focus on the tokens of the projects that host them. Two very different paths, which intersect precisely with NFTs: tokens we will continue to hear about even when the hype in the non-specialized press has finally faded.

A background noise that does not allow everyone to understand the actual functioning of these circuits and this technology. A noise that we have decided to eliminate with this in-depth analysis, with a technical and financial mix of one of the most interesting realities - together with decentralized finance, from the world of blockchains and cryptocurrencies.

NFT FAQ: Common Questions and Answers on Non-Fungible-Tokens

What are NFTs?

They are unique and non-fungible tokens, which represent the right of ownership on a given digital asset. They can be created, sold and bought.

Can you invest in NFTs?

Theoretically we can speculate both on NFTs in the strict sense, and invest in the tokens of the blockchains that support them. Our in-depth analysis indicates the best projects of the moment.

Are NFTs a Scam?

No. They are a serious and reliable technology, which are already used by many large companies. But be careful, it is always better to turn only to reliable marketplaces.

What can be exchanged via NFT?

Whatever is digital and tokenized. We can choose to buy an image, a video, a song, but also a digital card. Or even virtual goods in equally virtual worlds.

What are the best blockchains that support NFT?

It depends on the type of NFT. We have selected seven different projects in our guide, with extensive insights. Overall, there are 30 blockchains that support NFT in our guide.

HOW TO INVEST IN NON-FUNGIBLE TOKENS (NFTS), THE NEW CRYPTO NICHE

How to invest in non-fungible tokens (NFTs), the new niche that has arisen within the cryptocurrency market that is attracting interest.

NFTs have been around for a few years and one of the first interesting decentralized applications to have made them known is CryptoKitties, cute digital kittens made unique by a smart contract on the Ethereum Network that, starting from 2017, have been sold.

For many these are only tokens suitable for crypto art (cryptographic art), but in reality, this is a reductive vision of NFTs and we'll explain why immediately, providing a broad definition of what a non-fungible token (NFT) is, and how it is recognized.

WHAT IS A NON—FUNGIBLE TOKEN (NFT)?

A non-fungible token (NTF) "is used to identify something or someone in a unique way," the developers of the Ethereum Foundation explain. NFTs, in other words, uniquely represent a digital or real-world object, and serve as certificates for verifying the authenticity and possession of the asset through a blockchain network (source: Binance Academy).

NFTs are born on the Ethereum platform, where they are regulated through the ERC-721 standard, ERC-721 Non-Fungible Token Standard, later improved by the ERC-1155 standard to combine fungible and non-fungible tokens on a single contract. On the TRON platform, however, the standard is a derivation and is called TRC-721.

These tokens are ideal for use on platforms that offer digital collectibles, access keys, lottery tickets, seating for concerts and / or sports competitions, etc.

Precisely because they are not only used for CryptoArt, NFTs need a standard that identifies their characteristics from a purely technical point of view, and which first of all allows developers to program them correctly.

The technical feature that makes them unique compared to other tokens, for example the ERC-20, is the "visual" that can be associated with them. The ERC-721s are in fact equipped with a uint256 variable called tokenId. This variable allows a dApp equipped with a "converter" to use the tokenId variable as an input to output an image of something deemed to be interesting, such as weapons, digital paintings, kittens, zombies, skills (source: Ethereum Docs).

We understand, therefore, that we go far beyond crypto art understood as a digital or digitized work of art preserved in an ERC-721 smart contract (ERC-1155 or TRC-721). Think, for example, of the world of video games. Each gamer will be able to have their own personal and unique armor compared to that possessed by others, each will be able to choose and buy a personalized sword.

THE MOST POPULAR AND ADVANCED NFT PROJECTS

To understand the possibilities of non-fungible tokens (NFTs), let's briefly discover some of the most popular projects that have captured the hearts of early adopters in recent years.

CryptoKitties: essentially started as a game where you can collect adorable kittens designed by artists or other users. Kittens can be bought and sold with other members of the community, a bit like you did when you were a kid with stickers, but in this case the money you get is real. In addition, the user can play in KittyVerse.

Sorare: dedicated to the world of football, the game is halfway between fantasy football and the collector's album. Users, in fact, buy the digital cards depicting the football champions (126 teams represented), and make up their squad. They then compete with others based on the weekly performance of individual footballers. Also, in this case there is a dedicated marketplace where you can buy and sell digital cards linked to a smart contract.

The Ethereum Name Service (ENS): why limit yourself to the world of HTTP, if you can have an asset linked to the Ethereum blockchain? With ENS it becomes possible to decentralize the name of a website, a wallet and much more.

Unstoppable domains: the company behind this dApp allows the user to generate blockchain domains to replace cryptocurrency addresses with a name that is easier to memorize. The service can also be used to create censorship-resistant websites.

Gods Unchained card: the world of collectible cards has moved to Ethereum. This trading card game (TCG) has assets of $7 million in terms of trade. In addition to playing with collectible cards, in fact, collectors can sell them for profit.

These examples make it easier to understand what non-fungible tokens (NFTs) are and how they, in addition to fueling the crypto art market, can do much more.

NFT AND INVESTOR INTEREST

We have explained what an NFT is and briefly presented some of the most successful projects of recent years, but where does the economic interest lie for the investor?

This is where artistic NFTs (Kryptokitties, Gods Unchained, digital works of art and others) come into play, which can be bought from a catalog or at auction and then resold later at a higher price to turn a profit.

Operating on the marketplace of each dApp is impractical for the investor, for this reason dedicated platforms such as OpenSea have come to the rescue.

These platforms are real NFT trading exchanges that have an economic value, or that hopefully will have some in the near future. Digital collectibles, domain names, trading cards, cryptographic art, etc. are on sale.

NFT TOKENS TO INVEST IN

Each platform dedicated to NFTs also has its own NFT that can be purchased and in which the investor can invest.

According to CoinMarketCap, 132 NFTs are available for trading, here the list, but it is certainly destined to grow.

Which NFT tokens to invest in? The market is immature, the advice is to study the individual projects and follow them to understand what the project presents and the most robust vision.

BEWARE OF SCAMS

In illustrating what a non-fungible token (NFT) is, we were a bit technical explaining that it is linked to an IT standard. This is because it is necessary to understand the underlying technical aspect if you do not want to run the risk of running into scam websites and / or false communities that offer NFTs that in reality are not as they appear.

How to understand if a project proposing an NFT smart contract is not a fake? As for Ethereum the complete list of non-fungible tokens (NFT) is on Etherscan: https://etherscan.io/tokens-nft.

Separate reflection is needed for works of art and real-world objects tokenized and sold as NFTs. Who guarantees their real uniqueness? That is, I could tokenize a work of art such as NFT on Ethereum, then on TRON and maybe also on Binance Chain, and try to sell each one as a unique NFT of that work, for the sole purpose of pocketing more money, obviously scamming the buyers.

Therefore, a problem of standardization of procedures and transparency emerges that even blockchain protocols alone cannot solve. The problem of Garbage-in, Garbage-out (Gi-Go), must always be taken into due consideration.

In conclusion

Non-fungible tokens (NFTs), respecting the multifaceted nature of cryptographic assets, do not fit neatly into a well-defined category, but are placed between decentralized finance, hobby and recreational activities of collectors, and cryptographic digital art (crypto art).

The sector is only in its infancy, immature and for now very "overbought". Be careful, therefore, because not all the works that today receive high prices will keep their price, including those jokes at Christie's.

FROM $2,000 TO $10,000 IN LESS THAN 10 DAYS WITH NFTS

I have thought for a long time about the title for this chapter. I usually avoid click-bait and although it may seem superficial reading, I believe that there is nothing wrong with transparently sharing the investment process and the exact earnings obtained.

If you are interested in learning more about the world of NFT investing, consider:

- Have a starting capital, even as Smooth as in this case (which, however, does not have to be all your savings!)
- Know what you invest in, so accordingly,
- Have an investment strategy,
- Be clear on the time horizon of the investment or speculation,
- Know the basics of art history,
- Know the author / artist,
- Learn about the crypto world, especially Ethereum,
- Get to know the NFT world,
- Know what it means to have digital ownership of a file,
- Know that, despite everything, you can lose money.

With the hope of having removed the "dupes" I can now describe in detail the investment process that led me to have a profit of 362.5% in a few days.

In this chapter you will find:

- What is an NFT?
- What is Damien Hirst's The Currency project?

- Analyses
- Earnings
- Losses and mistakes made

Disclaimer

Each analysis presented exclusively reflects the author's point of view and does not represent financial advice and should not be taken as a forecasting support on the future trend of the markets and financial assets analyzed.

What is an NFT?

A simple way to think about NFTs or Non-Fungible Tokens, in Italian non-fungible assets, is to consider them as digital files registered on the blockchain. This means that, thanks to blockchain technology, they cannot be copied, modified, deleted or manipulated.

 The difficulty so many people fail to attribute a value to a digital asset, such as Bitcoin, is because since the internet started, we have exchanged tons of digital material, but we have never really owned it.

The Internet has disrupted information but failed to disrupt value.

 Up to now, every work, song, film that could be digitized has been digitized with the consequent loss of the original copy. Whole industries have collapsed, and others have risen from their ashes in the face of this paradigm shift.

 A simple example to explain is the transformation of the music industry. With the invention of Napster in 1999, people were able to exchange songs for free in the form of digital files over the internet. The information inside the single file containing the song was exchanged, the value was not. This new technological paradigm undermined the entire industry for more than two decades and it never returned to pre-internet sales levels.

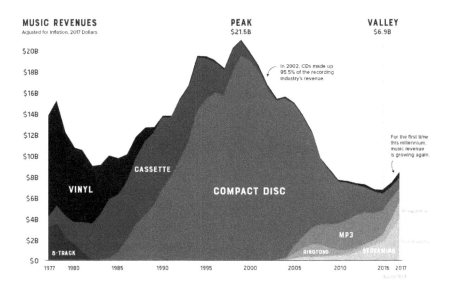

The person who saw this opportunity was Daniel Ek, founder of Spotify and former CEO of µTorrent, one of the most popular BitTorrent clients. Ek understood that piracy was not a matter of theft, but of access and from the ashes of CDs, Spotify arose.

Today, we are laying the foundations to build a metaverse, a digital universe, which has the same rules as the real world but with an extra gear. And it is in this new and uncertain environment, but also promising in my opinion, that the creative industry can have a new golden age.

What does the blockchain have to do with all this?

The blockchain provides marketability, liquidity and trust between two parties that do not know each other, giving users ownership and management of their digital assets, which are called Non-Fungible Tokens or NFTs.

What is Damien Hirst's The Currency project?

The Currency, Damien Hirst's first collection of NFTs, consists of 10,000 NFTs which correspond to 10,000 unique physical works of art that are stored in a vault in the UK.

The physical works, created in 2016, explore the boundaries of art and currency - when art changes and becomes a currency, and when currency becomes art.

The Currency challenges the concept of value through money and art. Each of the 10,000 unique hand-painted works are released as NFTs on the blockchain. Each work of art is uniquely titled and numbered (1 - 10,000). The titles are generated by a machine learning algorithm applied to some of the artist's favorite song lyrics.

The collector decides how to use his art / currency. Keep it, exchange it, change it, use it, enjoy it. After exactly one year from the release of the work, you will have to decide whether to keep the digital NFT or the physical artwork, both of which are works of art in their own right. Whatever the collector's choice, the other copy will be burned.

It is also an experiment for Hirst, as he too declares that he does not know what the market will decide in a year. Will collectors decide to keep the digital NFT, setting a fundamental precedent in the evolution of art and the concept of possession, or will the physical version currently held in the vault prevail?

Damien Hirst

Damien Hirst is a British artist, very controversial for his works, whose name has become synonymous with contemporary art. From a young age, when still a student at Goldsmiths School of Art, Hirst's production redefined the boundaries of art. Working primarily with installations, painting, sculpture and drawing, Hirst explores the complex relationships between art, beauty, religion, science, life and death.

Damien Hirst is famous for initiating the Young British Artist movement and for his controversial paintings, sculptures and avant-garde pieces. Like Andy Warhol, Hirst has always embraced the factory method of producing art. In fact, he owns a real factory in the UK where he employs artists, metallurgists and sculptors to produce his visions.

Analyses

When I learned that Damien Hirst, one of the best-known contemporary artists in the world, would release an NFT I immediately thought it was an excellent investment opportunity and that it would make sense to do an in-depth analysis of the project, of the possible return on investment. and the time horizon to which I would have liked to be exposed.

An original painting by Damien Hirst can be worth from a few thousand dollars up to tens of millions of dollars. Damien Hirst's most valuable work is the painting Lullaby Spring (2002) which sold for $19,213,270 on June 21, 2007. This shows that Damien Hirst's paintings represent a great opportunity for an investor, Hirst being an established artist with proven market value.

It is important to know the considerations made before purchasing:

1. Hirst is one of the best known and most valued living artists in the world

2. The Currency collection was conceived and created in 2016, the year in which NFTs did not yet exist, and adapted to the new trend of the moment. Which makes The Currency a beautiful artistic experiment but

at the same time one of the many projects started with the aim of riding the NFT trend to earn more money than with a traditional auction.

3. There were more than 30,000 unique applications and about 67,000 offers to buy The Currency works (meaning that, on average, each person who applied requested to buy about two works)

4. The supply, or the circulating number of works, is 10,000 NFTs which may seem like a lot but today it is the standard for NFT collections. However, it remains far more than Hirst's other collections.

5. Hirst does not have, and does not appear to have, the intention of cultivating an active online community (fundamental requirement for the success of an NFT today), excellent examples of this are the Bored Ape Yacht Club, Cryptopunks and PunksComic collections. All these projects involve the community thanks to economic incentives, such as new drops or giveaways, which attract people who want to hold the work and actively participate in the community and not scalpers, people whose purpose is to buy the work to resell it immediately. In support of this thesis, it must be said that Hirst receives 7.5% of the value exchanged at each sale of The Currency, this is reflected in the purpose of the project: to feed exchanges to earn from secondary sales without building communities.

In case I managed to be selected to access the sale of The Currency I had estimated 2 different scenarios.

The first scenario was that, if The Currency was positively accepted by the Smooth community of NFT collectors, it would have had an appreciation from the initial value of $2,000 to a maximum estimated value of $4,000-6,000, therefore about 2-3x the initial price.

The second scenario, in the event that the community that revolves around NFTs reacted negatively, I expected a difficulty in reselling the work (due to an illiquid market) and therefore a lowering of the value of 30-40%.

To reach my investment goal, to multiply the invested amount x2-x3, I therefore opted for a medium-long term time horizon of 6 months to 2 years, the time required according to my estimates to reach the market valuation estimated.

This is a chart that I kept an eye on during the first days of launch, it is noted that in the first 10 days, depending on the rarity of the painting, prices have maintained an average of $8,000.

The black line is the average, the dots are the individual trades in the secondary market

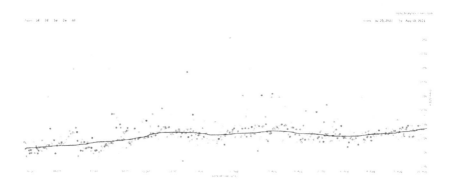

The price, only a few hours after the release of the work, was already above my estimate.

During the first days of August the NFT market boomed, with a parabolic pattern typical of speculative bubbles, and the price went from an average of $8,000 to $10,000.

This is a graph of the volumes moved by OpenSea, the largest NFT marketplace, from 2018 to today August 2021.

This graph instead shows the number of active users on OpenSea and the daily volumes.

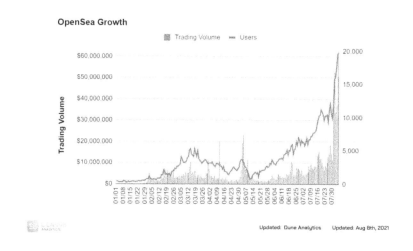

The following chart shows the typical trend of speculative bubbles.

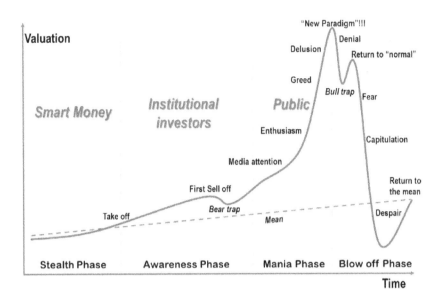

(Technical note, but important) At the time of the release of the NFTs in the wallets of the various participants, a high number of people were victims of a bug that made it impossible to move / sell the NFT to those who had a hardware wallet. In early August, the team from Palm, the blockchain that hosted the release of Hirst's works, was working to fix the bug. The resolution of the problem would have led a large number of works to pour into the secondary market with a consequent lowering of the floor price (starting price of the works).

My goals were largely achieved in a few days and my investment rules suggested I take home the $10,000 profit with a net gain of around $9,300 (7.5% of the trade goes to the artist in this case, Damien Hirst).

Remember that you have not made a profit until you have closed the investment.

In a traditional, liquid market, with divisible and fungible assets, I would have sold my investment in Smooth tranches spread over time, in the world of NFT it is impossible as the unique and non-fungible work is only salable in its entirety.

And that's where I missed a profit of around $30,000.

How I lost $30,000

Analyzing what happened in detail, we discover that on August 14 the floor price (starting price of the works) began to rise up to a peak of $38,000 (on average!) In the days of August 15/16.

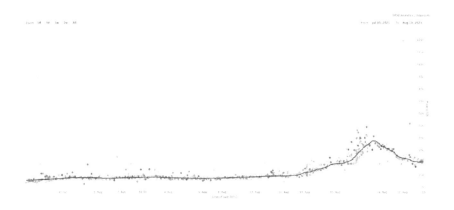

And so I asked myself, what happened in those days? What led to that price hike? Has anyone with big capital manipulated the market?

Thanks to the open, free but anonymous (often pseudonymous) nature of the blockchain I found a wallet worth $12 million to buy dozens of works by Damien Hirst on August 8 at a price of $8,000-9,000.

This, together with other speculative causes, may have sparked a rush to grab a work by Hirst, causing the price of the works to skyrocket. I use the term "speculative" as no fundamentals changed during those days in August.

So?

Will you find me dead in the waters of Fuerteventura because I left the investment too soon?

Not even for a dream, closing an investment in profit, whether it is 10% or as in this case 362.5%, should NEVER make you regret your choice.

On an emotional level, at first glance, anyone would feel stomach ache thinking of a loss of earnings of these proportions (almost 20x compared to the initial investment)

The rational reality is that we would all be rich in hindsight.

THE WORLD'S MOST EXPENSIVE NFTS SOLD AT AUCTION: THE RANKING

The fashion for NFTs has exploded in recent months, with auction sales of multi-million-dollar digital assets. Here is the ranking of the 10 NFTs (+1) for which the most money was spent ever.

NTFs, short for non-fungible tokens, are digital assets sold as collectibles or works of art that have a certain value based on their uniqueness. A GIF, an audio file, a video, a meme, a 3D painting, a video game collectible ... all of these things can be NFTs.

This term can also refer to the digital token registered on the blockchain which corresponds to the object sold and which certifies its ownership and authenticity.

NFTs have existed since 2017 but it is only recently that they have gained great popularity: in the last year the boom of NFTs has seen many of them sold for over $1 million each, with the most expensive sold for nearly $70 million.

If crypto art and NFTs will be a passing trend or the future of collecting only time will tell. The fact is that in recent times non-fungible tokens are on everyone's lips also thanks to events that have seen famous faces protagonists. This is the case of Emily Ratajkowski: the super model with a post on Instagram announced a few days ago that she will sell the NFT of the photo in which she is posing in her New York home in front of an old shot for Sports Illustrated Magazine at Christie's.

These days the NFT sale of the popular meme "Disaster Girl" made headlines, with the little girl who smiles furtively in front of a burning house. The protagonist of the photo, Zoe Roth, now 21, sold the non-fungible token of her original image for nearly half a million dollars.

In March, NFTs hit the headlines with the sale of the first tweet in history written by Twitter founder Jack Dorsey: a wealthy investor paid nearly $3 million in Ether to grab it. It is one of the most expensive NFTs in the world sold so far. Here are the others.

1. Everydays, 5,000 days by Beeple - $69 million

The record sale of an NFT so far is "Everydays: The First 5,000 days", the digital collage with about 5000 images created by the American crypto artist Beeple. The work sold for a staggering $69.3 million at a Christie's auction. The auction house revealed that the buyer is under the pseudonym of Metakoven, the founder and financier of Metapurse, the largest NFT fund in the world.

2. 9 CryptoPunk Series - $16,962,500

Cryptopunks are considered to be the first NFTs on Ethereum. It is a series of 10,000 24x24 pixel art images generated uniquely by an algorithm. Each CryptoPunk represents a different character. The average bid over the past year was approximately $61,600 per avatar.

On May 13, Christie's broke a record auction, selling a series of 9 rare CryptoPunks from the Larva Labs collection for nearly $17 million. In the series we find five "female punks", three "male punks" and one "alien" punk. In 2017, people who started selling their CryptoPunks were earning anywhere from $1 to $30. Now, with the tzunami Nft, CryptoPunk boast a total market of 280 million dollars.

3. CryptoPunk #7804 - $7.5 million

The most expensive single CryptoPunk in history? Cryptopunk #7804, a teal man with a hat and sunglasses smoking a pipe, sold in March 2021 for $7.57 million by cryptoart collector Figma CEO Dylan Field to a Twitter user.

4. Beeple Crossroads - $6.6 million

Another work by Beeple takes third place in this top 10. It is Crossroads, a 10-second clip sold for 6.6 million dollars that shows a giant Donald Trump lying on the ground naked and covered with writing on his body after having lost the 2020 presidential election.

5. Hashmasks - $16 million

Hashmasks are virtual works of art created by a team of 70 artists from around the world and managed by Suum Cuique Labs. The works, representing colorful, bizarre and extravagant masks, are inspired by the graffiti of the artist Jean-Michel Basquiat in New York in the 80s. It all started when crypto-trader Crypto Cobain decided to invest $200,000 in Hashmasks and let it be known on Twitter. In just one weekend, thousands of users purchased the 16,384 existing Hashmasks for a total of $16 million.

6. Grimes' War Nymph - $6 million

Canadian artist and musician Grimes, Elon Musk's fiancée, has sold her digital works for approximately $6 million. This is "War Nymph", a series of 10 pieces, some unique, others with thousands of copies, put on sale on Nifty Gateway on February 28th. The best-selling was a one-of-a-kind video titled Death of the Old, inspired by a song by Grimes. Part of the proceeds were donated to an NGO committed to fighting emissions and climate change.

7. NFT first tweet in history - $2.9 million

The first tweet in history, published by Twitter founder Jack Dorsey, in its unique version certified through NFTs, was auctioned for charity on Valuables in March 2021 and sold for nearly $3 million. Dorsey has pledged to convert 100% of the proceeds into Bitcoin before donating them to Africa Response.

8. CryptoPunk #6965 - $1.54 million

The second CryptoPunk on the list is #6965. The character in this case sports a funky cap and is the second rarest type after the alien. It was sold for $1.54 million in February.

9. Axie Infinity Genesis Estate - $1.5 million

We are in the field of digital real estate, which is gaining more and more popularity in recent years. The NFT representing 9 plots of digital land on Axie Infinity was sold for 888.25 Ether, or $1.5 million. This virtual land sale marks the largest NFT transaction of all time.

Axie Infinity is a decentralized gaming platform on the Ethereum blockchain that allows you to collect and train cute little ball-shaped creatures called Axies that live in the kingdom of Lunacia. A kind of crypto-Pokémon.

10. Rick & Morty, "The Best I Could Do" - $1 million

Justin Roland, the co-creator of the popular animated series Rick & Morty, has launched the first collection of tokenized artworks inspired by cartoon graphics. "The Best I Could Do" raised a million dollars at the Nifty Gateway auction. The most valuable piece, titled "The Smintons," sold for $290,100. Proceeds from the sale will go to homeless camps in Los Angeles.

11. Hairy by Steve Aoki and Antoni Tudisco - $888,888

 John Legere, the former CEO of T-Mobile, spent nearly $900,000 to buy the NFT of a 36-second music video made by musician, stylist and entrepreneur Steve Aoki in collaboration with 3D illustrator Antoni Tudisco. The piece is known simply as "Hairy" and features a blue and pink creature with glasses dancing to the notes of one of Aoki's pieces.

HOW TO CREATE AND SELL AN NFT

CASE STUDY 1

*Here is a little guide based on my experience
trying to sell an NFT.*

WHAT ARE NFTs, NON-FUNGIBLE TOKENS?

An NFT (Non fungible token) is the registration of a certificate of ownership of a digital object: an NFT can be a video, text, gif, book, music ...

In the last period there is really a lot of talk about it, especially after the artist Beeple sold one of his works for 69 million dollars. Without a doubt, NFTs are revolutionizing the art world. I have been obsessed with it for the past few weeks and so I decided to test myself.

This historic moment must also be remembered. And it goes together with other equally historic moments on the internet ... like ... like that time we downloaded the first song from Napster, or signed up for Myspace, or found our first-grade friend on Facebook or listened to our first ASMR ...

NFTs allow you to certify GIF, video, jpeg, mp3 and almost all other file formats existing in the world and considered as unique works. This technology allows you to create a new type of "ownership" for digital files that was not possible before. NFTs can be bought, collected, sold and even destroyed just like physical objects.

Thanks to the blockchain, they come with a transparent transaction and a price history that is visible to anyone with an internet connection.

CAN I SELL AN NFT?

The answer is yes, and these days I have decided to test myself and experiment. Below is my guide on how to sell an NFT using MetaMask (digital wallet) and OpenSea (marketplace).

WHAT CONTENT CAN BE CONSIDERED AN NFT?

Potentially everything digital. Although right now it looks like the digital art world is experiencing a crazy boom! We live in a historical moment in which there is a lot of freedom of action in this regard and everything that is art, songs, recipes, manuals, books, or ideas for startups is potentially associated with the world of NFT.

For example... a gif could easily be transformed into an NFT.

HOW CAN I CREATE AN NFT AND SELL IT?

I confess that I am poorly prepared on the world of cryptocurrencies, but from what I am experiencing, extensive knowledge is not required to be able to start creating an NFT and selling it online. There are only a few necessary tools that require the use of a cryptocurrency. I am experimenting personally and from what I have read on other sites, the two necessary tools are: a wallet that allows you to use the Ethereum cryptocurrency and a profile registered on any NFT marketplace.

In (theory) a few minutes are enough to set everything up. Here are the things to do to start selling NFTs.

- Set up an Ethereum Wallet,
- Buy a Smooth amount of Ethereum,
- Link the wallet to a marketplace that sells NFTs.

1 SET UP A DIGITAL WALLET FOR CRYPTOCURRENCY

The first thing to do is to set up a digital wallet (wallet) that allows you to keep the Ethereum cryptocurrency that we are going to buy (and the one we will get from sales) in a safe place. The wallet will also be connected to the marketplace that we will select as the place to sell our NFTs.

There are dozens of digital wallets, but I chose Metamask, which for iOS has a very simple app to use and a Chrome plugin that allows you to be faster when setting up a profile on a marketplace.

2 BUY A Smooth AMOUNT OF ETHEREUM

Yes, it would be too easy to use common currency. In order to begin the entire NFT sales process, the platform that you will select will require the use of a Smooth amount of Ethereum, which will serve as a bit of a guarantee that the profile is real and I believe also to cover the expenses of the platform.

3 CONNECT THE WALLET TO A MARKETPLACE THAT SELLS NFT

Easy peasy, once the wallet has been set up, purchased a Smooth amount of Ethereum (I invested $200.00), you can connect the wallet to the marketplace that you like best. Right now, I'm experimenting with two: Opensea.io and Rarible.com. It takes about twenty minutes to be able to create profiles, make transactions and check that everything is ok.

After a couple of weeks of experimenting, I can say that Rarible seems unreliable at the moment. They asked me for a fee to load an NFT, but the NFT was never loaded, while the fee was taken. I have read on several forums that there are problems and the platform is perhaps still too simple to be able to handle the insane amount of data that is starting to arrive. The uploading of my first NFT on Opensea, on the other hand, went smoothly, even if the fee required for the first upload was quite high. Once this obstacle is passed, everything should be much simpler and more manageable.

How To Earn With NFT

The goal for many is to earn something. Now the market is emerging, but most likely in about ten years, the majority of the contents that will be distributed online will be covered by NFT, if at this moment the art market is involved as a main player, in the near future it could be the world of literature, entrepreneurship, patents... To earn something, it is enough to be able to make good communication and place our content on the market. The process is the same as when we sell something on Ebay, or on any other marketplace ... so the same process, the same rules: marketing, communication, networking and that stuff 😃

Beeple's NFT work

Setting everything up was not difficult and inspired by Beeple, I also decided to launch my personal challenge and try every day to publish digital art content, taken from my hard drives, from the things I do, the videos or photos I take etc. Beeple approached the world of digital art in a methodical way, sharing and selling his works daily for years. An exercise in style that allowed him to improve and refine his skills, and then lead him to create crazy collaborations over the years and get to today, with the achievement of a goal that is truly almost impossible to imagine.

I like to try to do things, not to be left behind but above all to broaden my horizons. On what I will publish and in what form, I already have some ideas, but right now I just have to start.

CASE STUDY 2

How to create an NFT and how to sell it online

The guide to creating and marketing a digital artwork. Without expecting to earn a lot, at least in the beginning

Memes of kittens traded as if they were paintings, tweets auctioned, collages of images sold for tens of millions of dollars, specialized art galleries: more or less since the beginning of the year, digital works guaranteed by an NFT, an encrypted certificate protected with the blockchain technique, are the phenomenon of the moment, online and even in the real world.

The acronym stands for non-fungible token and indicates precisely the non-substitutability and uniqueness of the asset, but how do you create an NFT? Above all: how do you sell it, after creating it? It's simpler than you might think.

First the wallet, then the collection

The first thing to do is to create a wallet, inside which to keep both your NFT and the cryptocurrency that you will receive from a possible sale: the most famous and used is MetaMask, but we have found Bitski simpler. However, opening the wallet is not complex: you need an e-mail address, you obviously need to choose a password and then just follow the few instructions on the screen. It is not necessary to buy any Ether, the cryptocurrency of the Ethereum circuit, the most popular and widespread when it comes to NFT.

Once this is done, it's time to create an NFT: we relied on OpenSea, one of the few platforms that allow this operation at no cost. From the homepage, simply click on Create to start the procedure: the first time, the site asks for the combination with the wallet (which is why that is the first thing to do) and allows you to choose a name and a description for the Collection in which the NFT will go, which will be assigned a random image that can then be modified later.

Subsequently, by clicking on Add New Item, it is time to choose which image, video, audio clip or 3d model you want to transform into Nft: OpenSea accepts Jpg, Png, Gif, Svg, Mp3, Mp4, Wav, Webm, Ogg, Glb and Gltf no larger than 40 Mb.

The next phase is that of configuring the digital object that is being created: the name, a short description, a link to a page (which can also be the profile on a social network, a blog or even a podcast), the number of copies that you want to make and so on.

What can you do with your NFT?

After it has been created, the NFT can be given as a gift (only to someone who has a suitable wallet), shared in the form of a link or on Facebook and Twitter, modified (until ownership changes hands) and obviously put on sale. To do this, there is the Sell button at the top right of the page: after the click you can set how many Ethers you are willing to accept as payment, if you want to sell at auction or not and how many royalties to keep from the transaction.

Having established all this, all that remains is to wait, remembering that in the case of cryptoart it is not so much the work itself that drives up the price, but the author: unless you are Jack Dorsey, Beeple or the singer Grimes (in short: unless you are somehow famous), it is best not to expect big gains. Not immediately, at least.

Case Study 3

How to create, buy and sell your NFTs

If you are wondering how, you can create your own unique and customized NFT, here is another easy guide to follow.

Non-fungible tokens (NFTs) are unique collectible crypto assets. The first existence dates back to 2012, when the concept of currency, Bitcoin token, emerged for the first time. These coins were simply referred to as satoshi, that is, Smooth fractions of a bitcoin, marked or "colored" with distinct information that could link the coins to real-world assets. For the most part, however, colored coins have been used to create and trade works of art such as "Rare Pepe" digital cards on Counterparty, a peer-to-peer trading platform built on the blockchain.

With the introduction of NFTs, the way has opened for the conception and creation of new non-fungible token standards, a set of constituent elements of the blockchain that allow anyone to create their own NFTs, which can also be traded on principal exchanges such as Binance as well as that Crypto.Com.

NFTs can be used to represent virtually any type of real or intangible element, for example:

- Artwork,
- Virtual items within video games such as skins, virtual currency, weapons and avatars,
- Music,
- Digital papers set,
- Collectibles (eg digital trading cards),
- Tokenized real-world assets, from real estate and cars to racehorses and designer trainers,
- Virtual Earth,
- Video footage of iconic sports moments.

How to create NFTs

What may surprise you is that creating your NFT graphic, whether it's a GIF or an image, is a relatively simple process and doesn't require in-depth knowledge of the cryptocurrency industry. First of all, you will need to decide on which blockchain you want to issue your NFTs. Ethereum is currently the leading blockchain service for issuing NFTs. However, there are other blockchains that are becoming more and more popular, such as: Binance Smart Chain, Tron, EOS, Polkadot, etc.

What needs to be understood is that each blockchain has its own separate NFT token standard, wallet services and compatible markets. For example, if you create NFTs on EOS, you will only be able to sell them on platforms that support EOS assets. This means you wouldn't be able to sell them on something like VIV3 - a blockchain-based Flow market, or OpenSea which is an Ethereum-based NFT market.

Since, the largest volumes of exchanges are found on Ethereum, which can also be traded on Binance Excahnge, this guide will focus on the creation of NFT, whether it is your artwork, music or video on the Ethereum blockchain.

Let's start: what you will need is a personal Ethereum wallet that supports ERC-721 (i.e. the Ethereum-based NFT token standard), such as MetaMask, Trust Wallet or Coinbase Wallet and about $50- $100 in ether (ETH). If you don't know where to buy Ether, we recommend Binance.

Once you have created your wallet, you need to know that there are a number of NFT-centric platforms that allow you to link your wallet and upload the chosen image or file you wish to turn into an NFT.

Ethereum's major NFT markets include:

- OpenSea
- Rarible

- Mintable

Makersplace: this also allows you to create your own NFTs but you must first register to become an artist listed on the platform.

If you picked the top three in the list, OpenSea, Rarible and Mintable all have a "create" button in the top right corner. Below I'll show you how it works for OpenSea, as there is the largest NFT exchange market, but of course the guide also applies to the other sites.

Clicking the "create" button (ie create, circled in red) will take you to a screen asking you to connect your Ethereum blockchain-based wallet. After entering your wallet password, the site will automatically link your wallet to the marketplace. Keep in mind that in some cases it may be necessary to digitally sign a message in your Ethereum wallet, all of which is simply to prove that you are the owner of the wallet.

The next step on OpenSea is to click the "create" button in the upper right corner and select "My Collections". In this menu you will find in your collections the NFTs you have created, and from there, click on the blue "create" button as indicated by the red arrow below.

Once you click on the blue "Create" box, a window will appear that will allow you to upload your artwork, add a name and if you want you can include a description (description is not mandatory).

Once you have uploaded the desired image to your collection, it will appear as shown below (red). You will then need to add a banner image to the page by clicking on the pencil icon in the upper right (blue) corner.

Perfect: you are now ready to create your first NFT. Click on the blue "Add New Item" button (ie, add new item indicated with the red arrow) and sign using your personal wallet.

The site will show you a new window where you can upload your NFT image, audio, GIF or 3D model. On OpenSea and many other markets, you also have the option to include special traits and attributes to increase the uniqueness of your NFT. Creators also have the option to include unlockable content that can only be viewed by the buyer. This can be anything from passwords to access certain services to discount codes and contact information.

When done, click "create" below and sign another message in your personal wallet to confirm and complete the creation of your NFT.

The artwork should then appear in your collection.

How much does it cost to create NFT?

While it doesn't cost anything to create NFTs per se, on OpenSea, some platforms charge a fee. With Ethereum-based platforms. this commission is known as "gas" or Ether. Ethereum gas is simply an amount of ether required to perform a certain function on the blockchain. In our case, the required operation is to add a new NFT to the market. The cost of gas varies according to network congestion. The greater the number of people carrying out value transactions on the network at a given time, the higher the price of gas tariffs and vice versa.

Personal tip: Ethereum gas tariffs are significantly cheaper on average over the weekend, this is because fewer people transact on the network over the weekend. This can help keep costs down if you are selling more NFTs.

How to sell NFTs

Now that you've created your unique NFTs, how do you go about putting them up for sale? Nothing simpler. To sell your NFTs on a market, you will need to locate them in your collection, click on them and find the "Sell" button. Clicking on sell will open a pricing page where you can define the conditions of sale, and you can choose whether to run an auction or sell at a fixed price.

Ether and other ERC-20 tokens are the most common cryptocurrencies to be able to sell your NFTs. As described above, however, some platforms only support the native token of the blockchain on which they were built. VIV3, for example, is a Flow blockchain market and only accepts FLOW tokens, which is totally different from the Ethereum blockchain.

What are royalties?

By clicking on the "edit" button next to the collection image on OpenSea, signing the message always using your wallet and scrolling down, you have the possibility to program the royalties and select which ERC-20 token you wish to receive for the sale of the NFT. Royalties allow NFT creators to earn a commission every time the asset is sold to a new person. This has the potential to create lifelong passive income streams for artists and other content creators automatically thanks to smart contracts.

How to buy NFTs

Before you rush to buy NFTs, there are four steps you need to take into account:

Which market do you intend to buy NFTs from?

Which wallet do you need to download to connect to the platform and buy NFTs?

Which cryptocurrency do you need to fund the wallet with to complete the sale?

Are the NFTs you want to buy sold at a specific time, for example via a pack or art drop?

As described several times, some NFTs are only available on specific platforms. For example, if you want to buy NBA Top Shot packages, you'll need to open an account with NBA Top Shot, create a Dapper wallet, and fund it with USDC stablecoins or supported fiat currency options. You will also have to wait for one of the card packs to be announced and try your luck trying to purchase them before they run out.

Pack and art drop are becoming more and more common as a way to sell scarce NFTs to a hungry shopper audience. These normally require users to sign up and fund their accounts in advance so as not to miss the opportunity to purchase NFTs when they are released to the market. Packages created and custom images can be completed in seconds, so you need to have everything ready in advance.

Where to buy NFTs

Here is a list of the most popular NFT markets to date:

- OpenSea
- Rarible
- SuperRare
- Nifty Gateway
- Foundation
- Axie Marketplace
- BakerySwap
- NFT ShowRoom
- VIV3

Is now a good time to enter the non-fungible token market?

Messari analyst Mason Nystrom predicts the NFT market will exceed $1.3 billion by the end of 2021, as more artists, brands and icons crowd the space to create their own signature tokens. As time goes by, there will be more and more blockchains competing to produce even better NFT services and a growing range of platforms to choose from, now that we are at the beginning it is definitely a great time to get involved.

CRYPTOPUNK, ETHEREUM'S COOLEST NFT PROJECT

The market for cryptographic collectibles issued as non-fungible tokens, usually known by the acronym NFTs, has exploded especially in these first nine months of 2021, with 2.5 billion dollars in transaction volume. The boom has also seen NFT enthusiasts rediscover some of the earliest non-fungible tokens, pushing the value of these cryptographic collectibles to hitherto unknown levels. One of these early NFT projects is CryptoPunk - a set of randomly generated pixel-based avatars. Some of the rarest and most desirable CryptoPunks have sold for millions of dollars.

But let's start from the basics: what are CryptoPunks? Created by development studio Larva Labs, CryptoPunk is a series of 10,000 images tokenized as NFTs on the Ethereum blockchain. An NFT is effectively a deed of ownership of a digital item, and in this case, holding a CryptoPunk NFT means that you are the sole owner of a one-of-a-kind pixel avatar.

CryptoPunk was released for free in 2017. Ethereum's ERC-721 non-fungible token standard wasn't even a concrete thing at the time, and Larva Labs' two-person team released them as an experiment. Ethereum wallet owners bought the 9,000 CryptoPunk released to the public, while Larva Labs kept the other 1,000 for themselves.

The volume of transactions around NFTs then gradually increased over the next three years, but it wasn't until late 2020 and especially early 2021 that demand skyrocketed for these digital collectibles, leading to sales. Multimillion-dollar NFTs and auctions at Christie's and Sotheby's. But what's so special about these CryptoPunks? One of the main characteristics driving the demand for CryptoPunk is that they are among the oldest NFT designs around and the first set of randomly generated profile images, they have inspired a growing tide of NFT sets of profile images and even has some owners of high profile, like rapper Jay-Z and influencer and investor Gary Vaynerchuk.

Additionally, there are clear differences that make some CryptoPunk more desirable and valuable for collectors. Alien avatars are the rarest of the randomized images, and as such, alien CryptoPunks are among the most expensive NFTs sold to date. Drawings of monkeys and zombies are also in demand. But how to buy them? All CryptoPunks are visible on OpenSea, the main secondary market for NFT, but can only be purchased through the Larva Labs website.

For access you will need to have an Ethereum cryptographic portfolio, through which to bid, buy and sell CryptoPunk through the official website. Helpfully, Larva Labs has a handy tracker that lets you see all punks listed in order of price, from cheapest to most expensive.

What are the prospects for CryptoPunk? There is no way to tell if the current level of demand will continue, but the entry-level price for CryptoPunks is currently continuing to rise. The minimum price reached $100,000 in early August 2021 and surpassed $150,000 a few days later, while it is now well over $200,000. Even a "classic" financial services giant like Visa became the unlikely owner of a CryptoPunk in late August 2021, calling the NFT a "historical trading artifact" and suggesting that "NFTs will play an important role in the future of selling retail, social media, entertainment and commerce".

Larva Labs will obviously no longer release any more CryptoPunks, as much of their appeal is that they are limited in offering and are among the oldest NFTs around. Instead, the company began moving on to other projects, such as 2021 Meebits, a set of 20,000 3D voxel avatars created in the same spirit as CryptoPunk.

THE 5 MOST POPULAR BLOCKCHAIN AND NFT GAMES IN 2021

We have collected the 5 most popular NFT games in 2021:

- Axie Infinity
- Sorare
- F1 Delta Time
- CryptoKitties
- Evolution Land

Our list of the most popular NFT games allows you to (potentially) earn cryptocurrencies by playing online.

The NFT space continues to grow dramatically and the online gaming market participates gratefully. We now have more game projects that tokenize their game assets, making them usable in the game and tradable as cryptocurrencies.

In this chapter, you will learn about popular NFT games that you can start playing right away.

- Axie Infinity
- Sorare
- F1 Delta Time
- CryptoKitties
- Evolution Land

AXIE INFINITY

Axie Infinity is a decentralized strategy game where users collect, breed and trade fantastic creatures called Axies.

Modeled after popular games like Pokemon, the game focuses on managing Axies and preparing them for battles against creatures known as Chimera* in a digital animal universe called Lunacia*.

All Axies are NFTs and each has four defining attributes: Health, Morale, Speed, and Skill, which define each Axie's role in battles.

Using Smooth Love Potions (SLPs), you can breed your Axies, increasing your NFT base. SLPs can be earned as a reward for winning battles or purchased on decentralized exchanges such as Uniswap. And like other NFT games, Axies, SLPs and other used NFTs can be sold in the in-app NFT market or popular markets like OpenSea.

Axie Infinity appeared in the news last month for selling nine parcels of land for $1.5 million in their upcoming virtual space. The Ethereum-based game registers up to 5,000 new users weekly, with weekly volumes approaching $1.8 million.

SORARE

Sorare allows you to play fantasy football using your five-player team's digital cards and earn rewards based on their performance in real life.

By now you've probably heard of Sorare, one of the best-selling NFTs on the market today.

Sorare is the leading NFT game for football, the most popular sport in the world. The game will appeal to soccer fans looking to take on team managerial roles as they continue to collect tokenized soccer cards.

There are two categories of trading cards that you can use to compete in different leagues: common and tokenized.

Community cards are free cards that are given to you at the beginning to build your team. Tokenized cards are Rare, Super Rare and Unique. They have a limited supply of - 100, 10 and 1 units per player, respectively. Tokenized cards can be used to compete with other users in higher leagues or traded on ETH compatible markets. For example, the Cristiano Unique card sold for over $100,000 a few weeks ago.

They are officially licensed with over 120 clubs and AC Milan, the popular Italian football club, is the most recent to join the game. Sorare records up to $4M weekly volume.

F1 Delta Time

F1 Delta Time is a Formula One game where users can participate in racing tournaments using digital collectibles. Collectibles include cars, trinkets, race tracks, drivers and tires. They are available in different racing qualities and are minted in limited quantities.

Tradable collectibles are also available in rarity levels. There are Common, Epic, Legendary, and Apex, which can be purchased using REVV, the native utility token. Tokens can be used for tournaments or sold on secondary NFT markets for potential earnings.

F1 Delta Time is doing a great job attracting Formula 1 fans to the NFT space. The platform records more than $1 million in weekly trading volumes and up to 1,000 new users weekly.

CRYPTOKITTIES

CryptoKitties is an Ethereum-based game with a simple storyline: collecting and breeding digital cats. With these two tasks come other rewarding adventures such as solving puzzles and creating collections.

At the time of this writing, there are more than 50K generations of these cats, each of which possesses unique attributes (called cattributes) based on the coding sequence. Prices depend on generation, generation 0 being the earliest and most expensive. The platform also features a marketplace where users can buy, sell or breed these virtual kittens.

The NFT rave all started with CryptoKitties in 2017 and looking at their numbers, it's safe to say they won't slow down anytime soon. The platform still records up to $30K in daily transactions and over 800 new weekly users.

EVOLUTION LAND

If you like virtual reality games, you will probably like Evolution Land.

It is a virtual cross-chain business game where you can buy and sell land, manage your space, grow crops and develop buildings. There is a total of 26 continents, each on different blockchains. Users can acquire land in these continents, farm, work on different constructions or hire other users to mine elements in their land.

Evolution Land players interact using avatars called Apostles. Apostles can be purchased through in-game auctions using RING, the native utility token, and bred to find rarer ones. Each apostle contains unique genes and talents that determine his abilities, such as mining, healing, research and combat. You can rent or sell your apostles to other users or distribute them for assignments according to your abilities.

NFT games are a mix of thrill and potential profitability. Playing these games to potentially earn cryptocurrencies requires knowing the game and how to win in order to receive cash rewards.

NFTs are digital and unique collectibles on the blockchain. Thanks to this functionality, they can be used in video games to represent characters, objects and other exchangeable elements.

NFT games have become popular in the Game-fi world as a way to generate income. You can sell your NFTs in-game to other collectors and players, and even earn tokens through play-to-earn models.

When moving your gaming NFTs, be sure to transfer them to a compatible wallet. Also, beware of the most common scams whenever you send NFTs to an NFT marketplace or to another user. Finally, carefully read the rules of any NFT game you play, to be clear about the risks related to potential losses.

NFT games are mainly present on the Ethereum network and Binance Smart Chain (BSC). Some offer collectible character fights like in CryptoBlades and Axie Infinity, while others use collectible cards like in Sorare.

Binance also offers NFT Mystery Boxes, which give the possibility to own NFTs with different levels of rarity. These Boxes are included in some Collections issued in collaboration with some NFT games.

Since their inception with the boom of CryptoKitties, NFT games have developed and started offering play-to-earn game models. Game-Fi, is the term that defines these NFT games, which combines the world of finance with that of gaming, providing players with the opportunity to earn while they play. You no longer need to win, find or breed a rare collectible worth thousands of dollars. Players can now experience more game models that touch on more themes than just the collectible animal world.

An NFT is not fungible. This means that each token is unique and can never be exchanged for another identical token. You can exchange 1

BTC (bitcoin) for any other 1 BTC. This is not possible with an NFT, even if it represents a crypto art object released in a series with multiple versions. Each NFT will always remain unique. In this case, the metadata of each NFT will be different, just like in a series of numbered prints.

How do NFT games work?

NFT games are different from keeping simple collectibles in your wallet. An NFT game will leverage NFTs in rules, game mechanics and player interactions. For example, a game could represent your character or avatar using an NFT. The digital items you find throughout the game could also be NFTs, which you can then trade with other players to make a profit. A new model of the play-to-earn type, also allows you to generate revenue thanks to NFT games, but more on that later.

So technically how do NFTs integrate and implement in a gaming environment? To exchange, create and implement NFTs within a game, developers create smart contracts that form the rules on how such NFTs can be used. Smart contracts automatically execute lines of code on a blockchain.

For example, CryptoKitties has a Smooth number of smart contracts that structure the game. The most famous is the geneScience contract which determines the random mechanics that generate new cats. Initially, the developers kept this piece of code hidden. Some players interested in understanding this dynamic have also created some tools to analyze the probabilities that would lead to the birth of new cats with particular traits. With this information, players could optimize their chances of developing a rarer breed that is worth more.

What are play-to-earn NFT games?

Play-to-earn NFT games offer users the ability to earn by playing. Typically, a player is rewarded with tokens and occasionally with NFTs; the gain is proportional to the playing time. Earned tokens are often needed as part of the game's crafting process.

Gaming token earning is usually the more reliable method of the two, as tokens can be earned consistently by playing, while NFT drops are more based on chance. The play-to-earn model has been particularly popular with users in low-income countries, as an alternative or support to their income or social security aid.

Axie Infinity has become one of the best-known play-to-earn games. The game requires an initial investment to purchase three Axies, or you can receive a free scholarship from another player. Once you have a Starter Team and have started completing tasks and challenges, you can earn Smooth Love Potion (SLP), an ERC-20 token that can be traded on various exchanges.

Players use SLP to breed new Axies, creating an entire economy. Axie Infinity became especially popular in the Philippines, where many users started living using this play-to-earn model. Many players make between $200 and $1000 (USD) per month, and others even more, depending on the market price and time invested.

What are in-game NFTs?

In-game NFTs offer another way to generate income by playing NFT games. Instead of earning a token ERC-20 fungible as SLP in Axie Infinity or SKILLS in CryptoBlades, in this case gains of NFT representing objects of collection. This gaming mechanism is the traditional one for generating income with NFT games. Items will have a different value based on their aesthetics, rarity or usefulness in the game.

CryptoKitties is an example that relies solely on the collectability of NFTs within the game. There is no way to keep playing and earn a steady income, without taking into account the variable related to chance. Many of the recent NFT video games offer a combination of play-to-earn and in-game NFT models.

How Do NFT Games Make Profits?

The amount of money you can earn playing an NFT video game will depend on the type of game and the market demand. The money you get comes from other users who value NFTs or cryptocurrencies earned while playing. You will need to cash in on the profits by selling your assets on the market, on an exchange or through an auction. In NFT games, the value is calculated based on the collectability of an NFT or token or their usefulness in the game. These two factors also lead to a lot of speculation.

Can I lose money playing NFT games?

It is possible to lose money by playing NFT games. The exact amount depends on the type of game, its mechanics and the value of the NFTs you are using. In this case, losing money does not necessarily mean that you have been scammed. Since NFTs are a speculative category and their value depends on what other people attribute, your losses also depend on market forces. Like any crypto investment, you only spend what you can afford to lose.

Can I lose my NFTs?

Given the value some NFTs have, it is a common fear of losing them while playing or interacting with the blockchain. Whether you bought your NFTs or earned them in-game, you need to make sure you keep them safe. In short, it is possible to lose your NFTs if you are not careful. However, the chances of losing them are minimal if you follow the best practices we will describe later.

Here are some ways you could incur the loss of your NFTs:

1. You try to transfer an NFT from your wallet to another that does not support the standard of the token you are transferring.

2. You are the victim of a scam or fraud and you send your NFT to a scammer.
3. You authorize a malicious smart contract to access your wallet, which steals your NFT.
4. You lose an NFT as part of the rules of a game.

Except in the last case, you can avoid the situations described above by improving your knowledge related to NFTs, blockchain technology and scams in general. Just as you wouldn't use PayPal or your internet banking login portal without first informing yourself properly, the same goes for NFTs. To make sure you don't lose your NFTs, you need to:

1. Have confirmation and certainty not to fall into a scam when sending your NFT to another wallet.
2. Know the types of tokens and blockchains supported by your wallet or platform. ERC-721 and ERC-1155 are the most common NFT token protocols on Ethereum and BEP-721 and BEP-1155 are the most common on Binance Smart Chain (BSC). Always make sure you send them to the correct address and never assume their compatibility.
3. Interact only with smart contracts of reputable projects you can trust. If you allow a smart contract to interact with your wallet, be aware of the risk that that contract could remove funds from your wallet.
4. Check carefully the rules of the game you are playing. Some NFT games allow you to trade with other users or use pay-as-you-go NFTs. They could be items or potions, for example. Familiarize yourself with the game to avoid unwanted surprises.

Popular NFT games

There is a wide range of NFT games available mostly on BSC and Ethereum. Some offer more traditional gaming experiences and others rely primarily on the collectability of NFTs.

Axie Infinity

As we've already mentioned, Axie Infinity follows a Pokemon-like pattern with collectible creatures and battles. Axie Infinity is on the Ethereum blockchain and provides users with potential income based on trading Smooth Love Potions (SLP), Axies and Axie Infinity Shards (AXS). SLP and AXS are both available for trading on Binance.

Sorare

Sorare is a fantasy football game where footballers can be collected and exchanged. You create a five-player soccer team, where you can also use the cards available for free if you are starting out or can buy other tokenized cards. You can earn points and level up based on each match you win, the goals you score or other events you complete.

Gods Unchained

Gods Unchained is an NFT trading card game available on Ethereum, it is similar to Magic The Gathering or Hearthstone. Players build decks with different powers and strengths to challenge other players. When you win, you find in-game items to use or sell. If you win Ranked games, you can start earning Flux which allows you to create powerful NFT cards. You can then make a profit by selling these cards or reinvesting them in new cards and continuing the process.

Binance NFT Collection

Binance NFT Marketplace offers an NFT gaming experience through partnerships with NFT Mystery Box and Collection. These partnerships range from those with digital artists to NFT games. Each purchasable Mystery Box contains a random NFT with a different rarity than a Collection. You can open the box to reveal the NFT or sell it without opening it.

 The NFT Collections contain several NFTs and Mystery Boxes centered around a theme or project. Some of the most popular projects so far have been Game-fi Mystery Box Collections. Let's take a look at some:

1. The MOBOX Collection. MOBOX is a BSC-based gaming platform that combines DeFi yield farming with NFTs. The Collection includes NFT Mystery boxes containing MOMO NFTs with a random power hashing to be used on the MOBOX platform. The more hashing power an NFT has, the more collectible this MOMO is in MOBOX games.
2. The My Neighbor Alice Collection. My Neighbor Alice is a game set in a virtual world with aesthetic objects represented in the form of NFTs. While the game assets contained in the Mystery Boxes of the Collection are cosmetic items only, users can enhance and price them in the secondary market.

NFT games take digital collectibles and create rules for players to interact with other participants' NFTs. While some people like NFTs because they can be collected, others want them for their usefulness. Many NFT games function as a trading card game, but not all collectors intend to take part in the game as well. Game-fi has created a new economy around NFT games, these have changed the way people can make money using NFTs. To earn, in this case, it is not just about luck and collecting, but also about taking part in the game.

....

GUIDE ON AXIE INFINITY - A LITTLE SUMMARY OF HOW BEST TO START

Platform: Binance

Minimum deposit: €10

License: Cysec

Very low fees

Exchange with other cryptocurrencies

To start

The first thing to do is to install metamask and create an account, where we will use metamask to manage all cryptocurrencies in Axie, like Axie Infinity and smooth love potions. In addition to buying your first 3 Axies.

You can click on the Axie help link, or on the description to install metamask. Click on download for Chrome ios or Android. Create a Metamask account.

Install metamask, add to Chrome and open it. Now, if you are new, click on yes, let's set. Create a wallet, and create a password for the wallet. In addition to the seed sentence, which is the catchphrase of your wallet, and you have to write it down somewhere, because you will be asked for it later.

With the metamask installed and the seed phrase somewhere safe, the next step is to send ethereum to your wallet. There are several ways to do this, but in my case, I use binance to buy ethereum and then send it to my wallet.

Depositing funds in Metamask on the Ethereum network

If you don't have an account with Binance, you can follow the steps below to create one.

The first thing to do is to log into your Binance account, make a deposit and buy Ethereum.

Once you have deposited the funds in your currency, go to markets, search for your currency. Here you go to sell, the red button.

With USDT in our balance, we need to withdraw it into our metamask portfolio. To do this, we need to go to the wallet, look for the tether cryptocurrency and click on withdraw.

Withdraw Ethereum from Binance

Now, open your metamask wallet and click on your address to copy it. With the address copied, go back to binance and paste the address, enter the amount and the network, which you need to enter ERC20. Check that everything is correct and that you have entered the ERC20 network and click on confirm, enter the codes and confirm the transaction. Please note that the ethereum network has a commission of approximately $6-7.

An important aspect is to always have some ethereum in your metamask wallet to pay commissions, as we will see later in Uniswap, and not use it all to buy some cryptocurrency.

Now, after a few minutes, you will be able to see your ethereum in your metamask portfolio. So, let's continue with Axie.

Buying your first 3 Axies

The next step is to buy 3 Axies, in the Axie Marketplace, to be able to play. Here, you will see what the Marketplace looks like, and we need to log in. You can log in with metamask as we are going to do, click on login with metamask, next, connect and sign in our wallet. We just indicate the name. We will have to activate the Ronin, but for the moment it is not necessary.

To finish the account setup, we need to enter an email and a password, and we will be ready once the email is confirmed.

Now comes one of the funniest parts, which is to buy the 3 Axies to start the game. With ethereum and metamask linked, we just need to choose the 3 Axies to start with. We will go to the Market and decide which ones we need. A tank Axie with a lot of armor cards is very good, as are healers. We click on plants that are usually tanks, and look at the stats.

I advise you to look carefully and not to buy the first board you see, even if it can be a bit heavy, take your time before buying your first 3 Axies and starting the game.

With our 3 Axies purchased, we can go to our profile to see that we really own these Axies, as well as see the transaction on etherscan.

Install Axie Infinity on your computer.

The last thing to do is to install Axie on your computer or mobile. It works on mac, Windows and mobile. In my case I'm on Windows. We open the window, extract and install the setup.

Now we need to log in, and click on install, then start install. Now we click on play and we will be inside the game. You will see that when you enter the game, your Axies do not appear in my Axies, but don't worry. Just click on sync Axies. Click on the Axies at the bottom left and synchronize the Axies. And you will see your Axies that you bought from the Market.

Now go to teams, my themes, new team, create a new team. We will place our 3 Axies, and we will have our team to start playing. Keep in mind the placement, where the tank is best placed in front of everything. And you can move the Axies wherever you want. Save the team, and you will have your team.

Now we can go play adventure or arena.

Installing Axie Infinity on iOS and Android

To do this, we will go to the guide of Axie mobile that we have seen, and click on download the application. Log in with your email, and now click on download for iOS. Now we open our email and we can download it. In iOS, we will need to install testflight first, as it is a more closed operating system than Android, where you will receive a code. With testflight installed, just click on the link in the email, and it will open in testflight to download Axie Infinity.

With the app installed, it works the same on ios or android, only on ios you need testflight first, it will ask you for a qr code to access the app. To get the qr code, go to Axie Marketplace, and at the top you will see a qr code, and click there to get it. You can take a screenshot of the qr and go back to the app. Click on choose from photo and select the photo. This will automatically register you in the game and you can start playing.

You now have Axie Infinity on your mobile. If you want to use it only on mobile, remember to sync Axie here too, or they won't appear. Go back to Axies, my Axies and sync Axies to be able to play from your mobile.

How can I get Axies with the Ronin wallet?

The game of the moment, without a doubt, is Axie Infinity, a game that mixes the fun of a video game with the world of cryptocurrencies. It is a revolution for video games, the possibility of making money by investing in NFT is available right now with Axie Infinity.

To start with Axie Infinity we need to buy Axies to form our battle team, these Axies need to be bought with ETH in our account. The process of getting to buy Axies can be a bit tedious the first time around, as you will have to register your accounts and so on. What does it take to buy an Axie?

For this process of purchasing our first Axies we will need to have 4 accounts, we will explain in detail how to get each of them and how it will work during the process. The 4 accounts in question are MetaMask, Binance, Ronin and Marketplace in Axie Infinity. Let's start with Binance.

Binance account

Having a Binance account is simple, this exchange has entered the cryptocurrency field and its inclusion has been massive. After the explosion of its use, the platform makes it easier and easier to access the platform and the section for buying and selling cryptocurrencies.

To create an account on Binance, follow the steps below:

Click on the following link https://accounts.binance.com

Select if you want to register by email or by mobile phone.

Enter your details and password and click on create an account.

After creation, we will be asked for a security check, we must enter all our real data. Next, we must send a photo of a document that validates our identity.

The Binance account will be required to buy ETH with the currency of your choice and send it to the MetaMask wallet.

Create a MetaMask account

The installation of this extension is quite simple, let's go through the steps quickly.

Go to the extension store of your favorite browser and search for "MetaMask".

Click on Download and the download will start automatically, after a few seconds it will be installed in your browser as an extension.

Enter the extension and click on the "Try it Now" button to proceed with the account creation.

Click on create a new account and enter your email and password. You have to make sure you save the passwords.

That's it, with these steps you will have your MetaMask Account created in your browser, access is simple, if you are not logged out just click on the MetaMask logo and you will be in your account.

Create an account on Ronin

The process of creating the Ronin Account is quite simple, similar to MetaMask, so let's take a look at the steps.

Go to your browser's extension store and look for the "Ronin" extension.

Click on the download button and the download will start automatically.

Wait for the extension to install and create your account, the process is identical to MetaMask, here you can have multiple Ronin accounts on the same device.

With these 3 accounts created we can now buy ETH and transfer it to our Ronin wallet to buy Axies.

How to buy ETH and transfer it to your Axie Infinity account

Here is a step-by-step guide to send your money from Binance to Axie Infinity account, follow the steps exactly and everything will be fine.

The first thing to do is to log into your Binance account and at the top of the screen click on the "Marketplace" option and then click on "P2P Trading".

Within the P2P market you will select the currency in which you will pay, it can be Colombian pesos, Chilean pesos, bolivars and so on.

Then select the payment method you will use in the other box.

We are going to exchange our currency for USDT which is the easiest way to exchange USDT for ETH afterwards.

Select the seller of your choice based on the rate and payment method, click on the green "Buy" button.

Enter the amount of USDT you wish to purchase and follow the purchase process, then Binance will give you instructions on how to complete the purchase.

Once we have our USDT we can trade USDT into ETH without any problems and at a good price. Once the transaction is complete, click on the yellow "Send to Spot wallet" button on the left-hand side.

We now need to log into our Points Wallet to continue the process.

Select the Trade option above and click on "Convert".

Then we select the amount of USDT we want to trade.

Select the cryptocurrency you want to trade that balance with and it will show you how many ETHs you will receive.

Click on the "Preview operation" button.

After confirming the transaction and accepting the amount to be received, click on "Convert".

Once we have our ETH balance in the Spot wallet, we need to transfer it to our MetaMask account. We follow the steps below to make the transaction.

We log into our Spot wallet on Binance and locate our ETH balance.

Then, click on the options given on the left in the "Withdrawal" option.

Copy your MetaMask account and paste it into the "Address" field that Binance will enable.

Select the "ERC20" network which is the ETH network, if you don't choose this network, you risk losing your money.

Enter the amount to be withdrawn in the other field.

We confirm the transaction information and click on withdraw, after confirming the transaction click on "Continue".

Enter the security codes required by Binance for each transaction and click on "Submit".

After a few minutes, the transaction will be confirmed on the Ethereum network, and you should have the ETH already in your MetaMask account. With your Ethereum in the MetaMask account, let's proceed to the Ronin wallet.

Now we need to link the MetaMask account with the Axie Infinity account.

Log into your Axie Infinity account in the Market.

Click on the MetaMask extension and look for the "not connected" option and click on it.

We select our Axie Infinity account.

After logging into your Axie Infinity account, select the "Account" section and click on the "Attach Ronin to Account" option.

A pop-up menu will appear asking for confirmation of the link, click continue and continue with the process.

Once we associate Ronin's account with our Axie Infinity account we proceed to buy the Axies.

In our account, click on the "Bridge" section.

Select the Deposit option.

In the first field we have to give our Ronin address, copying it from the extension and adding it.

In the next Assets field, we select Ethereum, which is what we want to deposit.

Then we select the amount we want to transfer to our Ronin wallet from Ethereum.

Confirm the details of the transaction and click on "Submit", a Smooth menu will appear and click on confirm.

When you click confirm, you will get a pop-up window from MetaMask asking you to confirm sending the message to the other wallet, click Confirm.

After confirming the transaction, we will have our ETH in the Ronin wallet to be able to buy Axies.

If you are a fan, you need to log into the Market and choose your favorites. Remember to always check their characteristics and abilities to choose a good team for the adventure mode and the arena.

Select the Axie, at the top right you will see the "Buy Now" button next to the price of the Axie.

In the pop-up menu that appears, confirm the transaction for the Axie in your Ronin wallet.

Click on "Go to my inventory" and that's it, the Axie is now in your inventory.

We repeat this last process for every Axie we want to buy and that's it, it's that simple.

Remember that the inclusion of the Ronin wallet is precisely to save us the taxes that were previously present when the game was hosted on the Ethereum network. With our accounts already linked, we can send and withdraw money much faster without going through such a tedious process.

How many dollars does it take to get started in Axie Infinity?

You will need about $900 to cover the fees that will be charged to us by Binance, MetaMask and so on. With this money we can buy our first 3 Axies once the money is reflected in our Axie Infinity account with what was done in the previous section.

Of course, we can have many more Axies but we can start with 3. In the shop you will see all the Axies available for purchase, select the one you prefer, check its skills and other statistics to confirm that it is a good choice.

Click at the top right on the option "Buy now" and that's it, you already have your first Axie, buy the other 2 and you can start this wonderful adventure.

How to Transfer from MetaMask to Ronin?

Transferring money to our Ronin account will allow us to buy Axies. Within Axie Infinity we want to transfer the money from our MetaMask account with no problem. The information presented below will let you learn the method step by step. The first step is to effectively explain it so that anyone can do it.

Before starting the process, we must keep in mind an important point. First of all, we need to have our two wallets linked: MetaMask with Ronin. With this step completed, all that's left is to follow the guide below.

We must have sufficient Ethereum balance in our MetaMask wallet. The fees we have to pay can decrease the amount of money received in Ronin.

Let's go to our Ronin wallet, just below our balance we will see the option "Deposit to Ronin." There we click.

A pop-up window will open with the message, "Unlock your MetaMask" which basically confirms that the DApp must be connected to the wallet in order to trade normally.

Unlock your MetaMask

At the top right of our browser, we need to click on the MetaMask logo and link the MetaMask wallet with the Ronin wallet. Once they have successfully connected, we can proceed.

Once we have completed the previous steps, go back to the Ronin page and click on "Deposit to Ronin". When you are redirected to the other window, no message will be displayed, this is a sign that you have done well in the last few steps.

Deposit to Ronin

Select the "Deposit" option and you will be presented with a form.

In the first option of the form, it must say "Send Ethereum to Ronin wallet." Now, click on the Ronin logo in the upper right corner of your browser and look for the option "Copy address" to copy our wallet address.

When we copy our wallet address, we proceed to copy it into the field that says "-", "-", "-", "-", "-", "-", "-", "-", " - "Ronin address".

Ronin Address

In the next field, we need to select the type of cryptocurrency we will send to our wallet.

We select the cryptocurrency in question, we have a choice between Ethereum, AXS and SLP in their recent and old versions. In this example, we will transfer Ethereum and select this option.

The next field will be the amount we will send, specify the quantity and proceed as follows.

We confirm the data we entered in the form, if everything is correct click on Next and then click on Confirm.

When you confirm the transaction, you will be presented with a menu on the top right where we need to confirm the transaction from our MetaMask wallet. In this mini form we will see the commission that will be charged to us and how much the total amount sent will be.

We confirm from the pop-up menu and it will tell us on the Ronin page that the deposit was completed successfully.

After this process, all that remains is to wait 10 to 20 minutes for the transaction to be confirmed in MetaMask and our money is deducted. After it's been deducted in MetaMask, the payment is effective in a few minutes in the Ronin wallet.

As the minutes go by, we will see the number of ETH transferred to the Ronin wallet. It is just a matter of waiting and not despairing. And that's it, with all the following steps you will have already successfully transferred from MetaMask to Ronin quickly and easily.

Opening an account

If you are new, you are probably wondering how to start playing Axie Infinity. That's why we have created a guide that will help you step by step. Here you will learn how to set up your wallet in MetaMask, create your Axie Infinity account and create your Ronin wallet as well as sync them all so you can buy your first Axies.

Create a MetaMask wallet for Axie Infinity

Before you start playing Axie Infinity, you need to have a MetaMask wallet, which you need to set up.

Create an Axie Infinity account

1.- First go to the Axie Market, click on "start session or log in."

2.- Click on login with your metamask account.

3.- You will immediately receive a notification from MetaMask to confirm the connection request. If the signature window does not open automatically, go to the location where the browser extensions are, as you can see in the image below, then click "Sign" 2 times and continue.

4.- Choose your account name and click on Save.

5.- Now we need to configure our email and password by clicking on Configure email and password.

6.- We fill in the data and confirm.

7.- They will send us an e-mail to confirm our e-mail with a 6-digit password that we write and confirm as you can see in the following figure.

Create a Ronin Wallet

1.- On the same page we click where it says Install Ronin Wallet or we click here.

2.- Click on Add to our browser and confirm.

3.- Click on the Ronin extension that has just been installed in our browser.

4.- When the wallet opens, click on Start.

5.- We will open a page that welcomes us to the Ronin Wallet, where we have to click on the first button if we want to open a new account or on the second if we already have one and we want to use it in this browser. In our case, since it is a new account, we click on I'm New.

6.- We put the key in the new Ronin wallet, confirm it and press Create wallet.

7.- We do the same as the metamask portfolio, reveal the 12 keywords, keep them in a safe place and confirm the passwords.

8.- In the case of the Ronin wallet, we have to insert the passwords in the correct order, which is random.

9. We update the page Axie Infinity and the only thing left is to connect the Ronin account with Axie Infinity market account, so we click Attach Ronin account, it opens a window of the portfolio and you sign to approve the link and voila, we will have our Axie Infinity account configured.

It is important to know that with the Ronin account you will have 100 free transactions per day and the wallet is optimized for the game, where you can see the AXS and SLP game tokens. The wallet also displays its ERC-721 or NFTs for Axies, Land Plots and Land Items.

Metamask

Ethereum was able to create a vast and rich ecosystem of dApps around it; however, using these dApps has always been quite complicated. Something has changed with MetaMask and its ability to simplify the use of dApps, thanks to a simple extension for web browsers.

User interaction with blockchain dApps such as Ethereum requires a bridge, and that's exactly what MetaMask does. MetaMask is a web browser extension or plugin that allows users to easily interact with dApps on the Ethereum blockchain. This is possible, because MetaMask acts as a bridge between the dApp and the web browser, facilitating their use and benefits.

Thanks to this, users can easily use these distributed applications, all in an integrated way and from their favorite browser. With support for Firefox, Chrome, Opera and Brave, MetaMask has brought the world of dApps closer to the general public.

But How was MetaMask started? How does it work? What advantages does it offer? We will address all of this below.

MetaMask, the birth of a bridge for dApps

The development of MetaMask is the down to two programmers, Aaron Davis and Dan Finlay. They were the ones who laid the first foundations for the development of MetaMask in 2016. The idea behind the project was simple and revolutionary. MetaMask would allow users to use their web browser to easily interact with their favorite dApps, quickly and securely.

To do this, MetaMask would use the Ethereum web interface and API, web3.js. This official Ethereum library would be the fundamental foundation of the world of possibilities offered by MetaMask. Thanks to it, it would be possible to create a proxy or a communication bridge between dApp, MetaMask and users.

The job proved to be a technical challenge, especially in terms of maintaining the security needed by its users. However, MetaMask achieved its goal: on July 14, 2016, its first version was presented. At this point, the extension has become available for Chrome browsers and derivatives. Later, its version for Firefox would be presented, allowing the same extension to be used in that browser.

MetaMask has since become the easiest way to access dApps through an easy-to-use interface. All this without the need to configure anything.

How does MetaMask work?

MetaMask works thanks to the use of web3.js, a library that is part of the official development of Ethereum. web3.js was started to allow the creation of web applications that could interact with the Ethereum blockchain. Thanks to it, web pages and extensions can take advantage of the power of Ethereum and its features.

In this sense, MetaMask was created to be a wallet for Ethereum and a tool for interacting with dApps.

How to install MetaMask

The installation of MetaMask does not involve major difficulties. Being a popular and proven browser extension, it is available in the extension archive or repository. In this way, you just need to access the browser's store and download it to use it in your favorite web browser.

Where can I use MetaMask?

Due to the wide popularity of MetaMask, there are many dApps that support interaction via this extension. Among the most popular dApps that you can access using MetaMask, we can highlight:

Decentralized exchanges. Bit2Me DEX is one of these advanced markets. This type of trading platform allows you to clearly exploit the great potential of blockchain technology, completely eliminating the risk of theft as it allows you to have control of your tokens throughout the exchange process.

Apps like CryptoKitties - buy your kitten and raise it as your best digital pet. CryptoKitties is one of the most popular games in the entire cryptocurrency world. You can buy, sell or trade virtual kittens and earn money thanks to it. Its integration with MetaMask allows you to make full use of the gaming platform.

Forecasting markets such as the Veil Market; this is a renowned P2P prediction market that takes advantage of the Augur, 0x and Ethereum protocols.

Services like Bonfire. Bonfire is an agreement between users to "burn" ETH with the intention of making ETH rarer and more valuable. Each contract commitment also gives the user the opportunity to be randomly selected for a reward in ETH. Commitments range from £1 to £5 depending on which bonfire a user commits to. 55% of the ETH promised to the contract is removed in a burnt coin. A burned coin is the process in which each coin is permanently removed from circulation.

Games like 0xUniverse; this is a fun RTS type game where you have to conquer planets and expand your empire across the galaxy which, like others, allows you to use MetaMask to interact with all its aspects.

MyEtherWallet type wallets; this renowned online wallet is also another project that allows the use of MetaMask. Indeed, the use of MetaMask is recommended to add an extra layer of security to the wallet; this is thanks to MetaMask's ability to store wallet information locally.

Is MetaMask responsible for the mass use of dApps in Ethereum?

CERTAINLY!

Thanks to the development of MetaMask, Ethereum dApps have experienced a boom in their use and public access. Making dApp use as simple as installing a dApp has empowered the ecosystem and made it easier for millions of people around the world to access it.

Advantages

It is created with the web3.js library, which guarantees you can use the full power of Ethereum.

Completely free software, so you can check your code and get security updates and patches very quickly.

Ability to store private keys locally ensuring maximum security of your cryptographic resources.

Allows the creation of portfolios via HD.

6 buying axies

To buy Axies, the first thing you need to do is log into your Binance account, deposit your funds, be it dollars or another currency.

Once this is done, go to the markets and select your currency pair against USDT (Tether). You can then buy Axies. Once you have selected your currency pair, you need to go sell, and indicate the amount you want to exchange your currency for USDT, and then buy Axies.

With the USDT purchased, you can return to the main menu to see that the USDT is already in your account and the order has been filled. Go back to the market and look for the AXS / USDT pair and click on it.

Players can:

Compete in PVP battles to earn leaderboard rewards.

Breed Axies and sell them on the market.

Collect and speculate on rare Axies, such as Mystics and Origins.

Cultivate the love potions needed to breed Axies. These can be sold on exchanges such as Uniswap and Binance.

Starting in 2021, players will be able to earn a government token, AXS, which represents a real portion of the game universe, as it has government rights and tax sharing built in. However, these missions are not of the "winner-take-all" type and reward each player based on their effort and skill.

Axie's mission

Axie was built as a fun and educational way to introduce the world to blockchain technology.

Guide breeding and genetics of Axie Infinity

In Axie Infinity, players can breed two Axies to create a new Axie offspring. Axie offspring come in the form of an egg, which turns into an adult after 5 days. Axie offspring can then be used to fight, raise new offspring or be sold on the Axie market.

Axie Infinity parent child breeding guide. Breeding Axies will cost you some resources. Systems are put in place by developers to manage the Axie population. This will prevent inflation and a potential collapse in the gaming economy.

What is "breed counting" in Axie Infinity? "Breed count" is the number of times an Axie has already raised and produced offspring. Axies can only breed up to 7 times, so an Axie can have a maximum race count of 7/7.

Axie Infinity: Number of Races of an Axie. Generally, Axies with a lower number of races are more valuable. Axies that have a 0/7 race count are called Virgin Axies. Note that Axie siblings cannot breed together and parents cannot breed with their offspring.

What are the costs of raising Axies? Breeding two Axies together will cost a certain amount of AXS and Smooth Love Potions (SLP). (Related

Guide: How to Earn SLP in Axie Infinity (Breeding Guide)) The higher the number of Axies used to breed, the more SLP is required. Here are the costs of the breeding Axies for each breed count:

Breed number SLP Cost 0/7 1 150 SLP 1/7 2 300 SLP 2/7 3 450 SLP 3/7 4 750 SLP 4/7 5 1200 SLP 5/7 6 1950 SLP 6/7 7 3150 SLP. As you can see, the SLP cost increases significantly the higher the number of spokes an Axies has. This is why virgin Axies and Axies with fewer races are more valuable.

How to breed Axies in Axie Infinity. Here are the steps on how to breed Axies in Axie Infinity: Go to your inventory. Select the first Axie you want to breed. Click the Breed button. Select the second Axie you want to breed with. Click "Let's Breed!" And confirm the prompt.

How to breed Axies in Axie Infinity for the offspring egg. After a few moments, the new Axie offspring egg will be in your inventory. How long does it take for an Axie Egg to transform into an adult Axie? Axies will take five (5) days to reach maturity, after which you can transform your egg to become an adult Axie. This can be seen in Axie's "current state" progress bar.

You can only see an Axie's genes once it becomes an adult. Morphing an Egg into an Adult Axie is free and incurs no cost.

What are Axie Genes? All Axies have a body shape and six (6) body parts. Each part of the body has 3 different genes: a dominant (D), recessive (R1) and a minor (R2) recessive gene. When breeding Axies, genes have a certain chance of being passed on to Axie offspring. Here are their corresponding chances: Dominant (D) - 37.5% chance; Recessive offspring (R1) - 9.375% chance; Recessive Minor (R2) - 3.125% chance.

What are the genetic mutations in the Axie herd? Aside from the possibility that genes will be passed on to offspring, there is also the possibility that each gene will mutate. A mutation is when a gene completely transforms into a different random body part that is not inherited from the parents of the offspring. There is a 10% chance for each of the twelve R1 and R2 genes to mutate. Dominant genes, however, have a 0% chance of mutating. This means that there is about a 1/3 chance that no mutations will occur and a 2/3 chance that at least one mutation will occur. Here are the chances of an Axie child having 0-6 mutations: 0 mutations - 28.24% chance. 1 mutation - 37.66% chance. 2 mutations - 23.01% chance. 3 mutations - 8.523% chance. 4 mutations - 2.131% chance. 5 mutations - 0.379% chance. 6 mutations - 0.049% chance.

Reproduction costs

The baby costs 4 AXS and a certain amount of Smooth Love Potion (SLP), depending on the Axie's breed count. The breed count is how many times the Axie has already produced offspring. The higher the breed count, the more SLPs you will need to breed again.

This means that if you have an Axie with a breed count of 2/7 and an Axie with a breed count of 3/7, the total breeding costs are 4 AXS and 1200 SLP.

Smooth love potions can be earned by playing. You can get them in the Arena or in Adventure mode. Check out this guide on how to grow SLP.

Methods of reproduction

You cannot breed siblings with each other. This means that if you use two parents to raise multiple Axies as offspring, then those offspring cannot be used to breed with each other.

To counter this, you can use Breeding Loops. Replay loops are strategies for playing endless generations, starting with just 3 or 4 Axies. There are two main approaches: Loop ABC (3 Axies) and Loop ABCD (4 Axies), as well as a transition shape of Loop ABC -> Loop ABCD.

In this guide, I'll show you the basics, all the way to the more advanced breeding. With a few tips and tricks along the way. Before you get started, here's what you need to know:

Number of babies or breeds

Each Axie can be bred a maximum of 7 times. Most breeders stop at 3 to 5 broods because it gets quite expensive, it fluctuates with the price of SLP. When an Axie has 0 breed, this is what we call a virgin axie.

Once your Axies have hatched, they will take 5 days to develop their offspring from egg to adult.

Costs to start breeding

To get started with Axie breeding you must have at least 2 Axies to pair, and some cryptocurrencies which I detail below.

Smooth Love Potion (SLP)

This is one of the parts needed to mate your Axies and the amount of SLP required increases with each farm. For example, 2 virgins Axies with spokes (0/7) would cost you 150 SLP to get the first child for each parent, in total 300 SLP.

As you can see in the table below, pairing 2 Axies with 6 or 7 races is expensive, this is only done by people when their 2 Axies are 100% pure with specific cards and they know they can sell their offspring for more than they cost.

RAISE 0 1 2 3 4 5 6

	0	1	2	3	4	5	6
0:	300	450	600	900	1350	2100	3300
1:	450	600	750	1050	1500	2250	3450
2:	600	750	900	1200	1650	2400	3600
3:	900	1050	1200	1500	1950	2700	3900
4:	1350	1500	1650	1950	2400	3150	4350

| 5: | 2100 | 2250 | 2400 | 2700 | 3150 | 3900 |
| 5100 | | | | | | |

| 6: | 3300 | 3450 | 3600 | 3900 | 4350 | 5100 |
| 6300 | | | | | | |

If you want to know the exact cost to raise your Axies. You can help yourself with the above calculator.

SLP

APN

Infinite Axis (AXS)

For each match you make, you will need 4 AXS Coins, which you can earn by finishing in the top 60 each season in Arena Mode or by purchasing them in an exchange.

So, to fill in the above, you will need:

2 Axies.

The amount of SLP per race each Axie has.

4 pieces Axie Infinity (AXS).

Genetic

This is the most important aspect you need to be clear about as a breeder. Since then, each Axie has different genetics passed on by its parents.

The dominant traits, abbreviated as D, and then there's the hidden genetics known as recessive 1 (R1) and recessive 2 (R2).

What is the percentage of genes children inherit from their parents?

Father 50%

Dominant (D) has a 37.5% chance of being passed on to his children.

Recessive 1 (R1) has a 9.375% chance of spreading to his children.

Recessive 2 (R2) has a 3.125% chance of being passed on to his children.

Mother 50%

Dominant (D) has a 37.5% chance of being passed on to her children.

Recessive 1 (R1) has a 9.375% chance of spreading to her children.

Recessive 2 (R2) has a 3.125% chance of being passed on to her children.

If we want an Axie with the Serious gene with these two parents we have an 84.37% chance that it will inherit it because we add the 2 dominant genes 37.5 + 37.5 + an R1 gene from the father gives us a total of 84.37% and if we want Carrot to shoot in this case, we would have 93.75%.

That is to say, that to have 100% our Axies must have the same gene in the same body part 6 times 3 from the father and 3 from the mother.

To see the genetics and simplify your life as an Axie breeder, I recommend that you install this Navigator extension.

Mutations: very little is known about the mutations in Axie Infinity, but it is becoming increasingly difficult to predict what can be achieved by the algorithm change made by Mavis in June 2021. Some speculation claims that mutations can occur in each of R1 and the R2 genes with a probability of almost 10%. There are no recessive genes to determine the class of an Axie, below you can see the types of classes and how to obtain them:

Main classes

There are 6 main classes for determining that each child has a 50% chance of inheriting each of the classes from his or her parents at birth. Thus, a Bird / Reptile pair would have a 50% chance to produce a Bird and a 50% chance to produce a Reptile. If both parents have the same class, the child is 100% ensured for this class.

Secret courses

There are 3 secret classes in the game, to raise one, your Axies must be as pure as possible (+ 90%) and even so you have a low chance that a secret class will appear, to find the right combination below I'll leave you with an example of what you need to combine to get these courses and what benefits each have.

If we mix a pure fish + a reptile = Twilight, and these are mainly used as reservoirs.

If we mix a bird + a plant = Dawn, and they are good beginners thanks to their speed.

If we mix a beast + a bug, that can come out = Mechs, and they are good at criticizing while being faster than most beasts.

Generational breeding

Axies cannot be bred with parents, siblings or half-siblings.

....

WHAT DO NFT PROJECTS DO WITH THE ETHEREUM THEY GET?

According to a recent analysis by the Nansen blockchain analytics platform, the majority of ethereum (ETH) coming from non-fungible token sales, at 52.3% continues to circulate among non-entity wallets, while a significant amount of revenue from primary sales is reinvested in NFT.

The team stated, for Cryptonews.com, that wallet entities are wallets that Nansen has labeled and attributed to a specific entity (e.g. OpenSea, Rarible, etc.).

Therefore, non-entity wallets are those that Nansen has not labeled and attributed to any specific entity, which means that a non-entity wallet could be an individual wallet or even just an entity that has not yet been labeled.

The analysis sought to provide insight into what happens to the cryptocurrency spent on NFT and how it affects ETH prices.

According to the report, a 17.7% stake in ETH used to purchase NFT at primary sales was reinvested in NFT projects, including mint and marketplaces such as OpenSea or Rarible.

ETHEREUM USED ON EXCHANGES

Nansen said around 10.4% of the cryptocurrency was used on decentralized exchanges, both as liquidity and for swaps, while 3.6% of ETH spent was deposited on centralized exchanges.

The analysis removes the flow of ETH to non-entities and evaluates the flow of ETH in the segment of the entity with greater depth.

"Nearly 22% of this flow is returned to OpenSea, presumably to purchase more NFTs," the report states.

Additionally, cryptocurrency exchange Binance "tops the list" in terms of centralized exchange deposits (CEX), capturing 13.75% of Ethereum's flow to entities.

The main decentralized exchange Uniswap (UNI) follows closely with 9%.

Nansen said "around 6% is also used for CryptoPunk-related businesses, possibly as capital to make a purchase."

Reinvestment of NFTs

Nansen concludes that the NFT industry remains identified by some profit-seeking practices, with the indication on the detected chain of founders buying for some projects.

According to the report, "such behavior may indicate continued wash-trading. However, there is a healthy distribution of NFT miners and the growing number of unique buyers and a genuine growth of the NFT community. Some projects also stand out for the reinvestment of primary sales revenues into NFT, under the governance of their community."

Within the primary NFT market, Nansen takes over 645 NFT projects and estimates that approximately 84,000 ETH (currently USD 261.77 million) have been deposited in ERC-721 NFT contracts since last June.

This constitutes the main "sales revenue" accumulated by the addresses that are the first to mint these NFTs, the report explained. About 75,000 ETH ($233.72 million) were transferred from these contracts. 573 projects have transferred ETH, while 72 projects have not yet touched the coins in their treasury, the analysis says.

That said, the company identified only 80 NFT projects that achieved primary revenue of 300 ETH (USD 934,872) and above, with average revenue of 10.2 ETH (USD 31,786).

Regarding secondary sales, Nansen said that:

"Representing the historical volume of exchanges along with the number of unique buyers since July, we can say that secondary buyer interest in NFTs started to dampen in August. Decreases in Ethereum exchange volume that could be indicative of prices of lower sales, while the decrease in the number of unique NFT buyers could indicate a lack of new participants entering the NFT space."

However, since its low on August 19th, there has been a strong rebound in NFT trading.

12 SITES TO BUY, SELL AND LEARN ABOUT NFTS

Marketplaces, digital art galleries, even the site where to obtain loans thanks to NFTs: the web rides the phenomenon of non-fungible tokens.

Among the tech news that will mark 2021 there are certainly the NFTs, the non-fungible tokens that have revived the digital art world, bringing an almost unknown artist (Beeple) onto the podium of the most quoted living artists, after an NFT of his work was auctioned for $69.5 million.

 The idea of a certificate of ownership imprinted on the blockchain has evidently made its way into the hearts of collectors, who until recently were reluctant to invest in digital, therefore reproducible, works. But on closer inspection, despite the recent explosion of the phenomenon, NFTs are nothing new. Indeed, a real ecosystem has developed around the concept of non-fungible token for some years made up of dozens of different sites and platforms with the most unusual uses.

Here are 12 to see closely what NFTs are and how they really work.

OpenSea

The world's number one NFT exchange was founded by Alex Atallah and Devin Finzer, a computer engineer who cut his teeth at Google. It is a kind of global one-stop shop that allows you to trade NFTs, create them, view data and inspect other portfolios.

His manifesto reads: "NFTs have exciting new properties: they are unique, probably scarce, liquid and usable in multiple applications. Just like physical goods, you can do whatever you want with them! You could throw them in the trash, give them to a friend around the world, or sell them on an open market. But unlike physical assets, they are equipped with all the programmability of digital resources".

Mintbase

Another market for buying, selling and minting NFTs. But on Mintbase you can find niche NFTs that are not found on other platforms. The site covers categories such as music, subscriptions, services, tickets, news, and photography. In November, it obtained a million-dollar loan from the Chinese Sino Global bank: a signal according to experts that the NFT market was about to explode.

SuperRare

One of the oldest NFT art markets. Its strong point is exclusivity: artists have to apply to start selling on SuperRare and there is a long waiting list. The most prized piece? The unpublished Time covers that have so far earned the magazine about 1.5 million dollars thanks to the purchases of NFTs.

Nifty Gateway

Launched earlier this year, Nifty Gateway is an NFT art platform that immediately carved out an important place on the scene. The reason? It is an offshoot of Gemini, the cryptocurrency exchange started by the Winklevoss brothers. Yes, the very ones who contended with Zuckerberg for the invention of Facebook (but the law proved him right and so they fell back on cryptocurrencies).

Rarely

The first NFT art market to implement, last July, a token that encourages trading. It is called Rari and allows the most active creators and collectors on Rarible to vote for any updates to the platform and participate in its management.

Nonfungible

Those who are passionate about NFT cannot avoid it: this is a site that has given itself the mission of monitoring the evolution and trends of the various marketplaces, with evaluations, reviews and news. Launched in February 2018, initially to monitor Decentraland transactions in real time, the project has progressively grown and is now one of the most visited sites in the non-fungible token ecosystem.

NftBank

For insiders, its killer app is an NFT wallet analysis and monitoring tool. Just copy and paste an Ethereum address in the search string above, to know all its trading operations in non-fungible tokens.

Nftfi

Another site for professionals whose use requires an expert hand. It is a platform for loans guaranteed by NFTs. Users can earn a return by lending Ethereum or Dai (a stablecoin) to other users who offer their NFTs as collateral or take out a loan in turn. Speculation is around the corner, so watch out. But the idea deserves a mention because it shows how this market could evolve (the conditional is always a must).

CryptoPunks

One of the first NFTs issued on the Ethereum blockchain, back in June 2017. In summary, it is a collection of 10,000 unique Smooth pixelated portraits of punk (hence CryptoPunk) made digitally scarce thanks to the use of the blockchain. Each has been algorithmically generated via computer code and therefore no two punks are alike and some traits are rarer than others. They also recently starred at a Christie's auction.

Nba Top Shot

Here they are, the famous NFT collectibles with the official license of the NBA, the powerful American National Basketball Association. Short videos and digital images of cult moments of American basketball which among others have already obtained the endorsement of Sports Illustrated and The Verge, according to which: "Top Shot is so far the best chance that NFTs, which are mainly the domain of fans of cryptocurrency, can become mainstream. More than 800,000 Top Shot accounts have been registered, with a turnover of 500 million dollars".

CryptoKitties

The first NFT project to go viral and is credited for wowing people about the potential. They are cartoonish cats to breed like a Tamagochi. At the time they made headlines because they literally invaded the Ethereum blockchain. But then no one would have imagined that we would go that far. Beeple included.

NFT CUSTODIAL VS NON CUSTODIAL: WHAT'S THE DIFFERENCE?

As the DeFi ecosystem grows, NFTs are becoming more and more popular. When trading or holding NFTs or other cryptocurrencies, you can choose between using custodial or non-custodial services. A custodial service owns the private key of your wallet and holds your assets in custody. The Binance NFT Marketplace is an example of a custodial NFT platform that can be accessed through a registered account.

A non-custodial service gives users complete control of their wallet and assets. Users can trade their NFTs directly from their wallets. This creates a market without the need for intermediaries. This feature is featured on Featured By Binance, Binance's non-custodial NFT platform. By creating NFTs on the blockchain, creators are establishing a direct relationship with their fans without the risks associated with platforms.

Introduction

Non-fungible tokens (NFTs) are in high demand across blockchain and DeFi ecosystems. There is already a lot of information about NFTs, but we often don't discuss the aspects of their custody. Who actually has full control over the NFTs you just created or purchased? It could be that you have less custody of your NFT than you think.

This concept may be familiar to you if you have already explored the subject of wallets and cryptocurrencies. In fact, these two options, having custody of your NFT or letting someone guard it for you, are both valid. It all depends on what you are looking for and what kind of responsibility you want to have.

The various scenarios in which you will find custodial NFTs do not depend on the wallet you choose and the platform you use to trade or create NFTs.

What is a crypto wallet?

A crypto wallet is an essential tool for maintaining cryptocurrencies and interacting with the blockchain. If you want to transact and use decentralized applications (dApps), you will need a wallet. There are two main features for each wallet: a public key and a private key.

The public key of your wallet is used to generate addresses to which you or other people can send crypto. Your private key, which you should manage exactly like a password, signs transactions and provides access to your funds. There are a variety of options to choose from when considering which crypto wallet to use. Keys can be printed on a piece of paper, accessed via software or contained in a hardware wallet.

These wallets aren't just for storing cryptocurrencies. Depending on the type of wallet, you can also save NFTs. You have probably used a wallet to send or receive digital assets such as Bitcoin (BTC), Ether (ETH) or stablecoin. But some wallets can also be used to store and transfer NFTs, these are tokens issued on a blockchain.

What is a custodial wallet?

A custodial wallet does not give you full control of your private keys. A third party (such as an exchange or custodial wallet service provider) will hold your assets for you. You won't be able to access your private key yourself, but that's not necessarily a bad thing. It all depends on your needs.

Given the decentralization of blockchain technology, you can permanently lose access to your wallet if you lose your private key. By having a third party to keep the private key for you, you pass this responsibility on to him. Even if you forget your exchange password, you will likely be able to log back into your account with customer service support.

However, don't forget that in this case, a third party has your funds in custody. Your cryptocurrencies will be safe based on how the third party holds them. That's why it's important to choose a reputable exchange or service provider.

What is a non-custodial wallet?

A non-custodial wallet is a wallet in which only the holder owns and controls the private keys. For users who want more control over their funds, non-custodial wallets are the best option.

As already mentioned, in this case, the responsibility of keeping the keys safe lies in the hands of the wallet owner. If the keys are lost or the backup seed phrase is forgotten, the wallet and the funds inside it can no longer be used. There are various non-custodial wallets available as apps, executable software, and browser extensions. Popular examples include Trust Wallet and MetaMask. You can also find wallet services, such as Tor.us, which allow users to protect their keys by logging in to their social profiles, thus making the process more secure and convenient.

Which wallet can I use for NFTs?

You can use both types of wallets to store your NFTs. However, make sure that the wallet used supports the type of NFT you want to keep inside it. NFTs can exist on several blockchains or even on one and there can also be various types of token standards. Each standard has different characteristics and rules, which define how tokens are created and used.

The most common token standards are:

Ethereum: ERC-721, ERC-1155

Binance smart chain: BEP-721, BEP-1155

Whether you intend to keep an NFT on a custodial wallet (such as an exchange) or on a non-custodial wallet, it is a good idea to always check the NFT token standard first. With this information, make sure your wallet supports the blockchain and token standard of your crypto object.

 MetaMask, Trust Wallet, and MathWallet are all non-custodial wallets that accept the most common NFTs you might typically use. In any case, when you interact with a centralized exchange, you will use a custodial wallet. The best option is to check the exchange's FAQs or website for detailed information regarding accepted NFTs.

How can I buy an NFT with my wallet?

The process you will use to purchase collectible NFTs will depend on two factors: the type of wallet and the marketplace you want to use. If you want to have full control when purchasing an NFT and want to keep it in a non-custodial wallet, you will need to use a decentralized platform for purchasing, such as Featured by Binance.

Decentralized platforms (non-custodial)

If you've used Binance DEX or another decentralized exchange before, you may already be familiar with a non-custodial system. A decentralized exchange does not require the creation of an account or registration. You usually make a trade directly between your wallet and the counterparty's.

NFT Marketplace (Custodial)

An NFT marketplace acts as a guarantor during the buying process. If you want to place a bid during an auction, you will need to send your funds to the platform to hold them as collateral. Once you have purchased your NFT, you can keep it in the custodial wallet or send it to another wallet.

Binance's NFT Marketplace also requires you to transfer funds to its custodial spot wallet to buy and bid for an NFT. Your Binance account must have crypto in it, since the site will not interact directly with external wallets.

How can I create or sell an NFT using my wallet?

Decentralized platforms (non-custodial)

The process of creating an NFT is called minting. To create an NFT, you need to link your wallet and upload your digital assets to an NFT platform, such as Featured by Binance. You can upload images, audio or video files along with some metadata (useful for describing your NFTs). You can choose to create individual NFTs or a collection, the latter consisting of a group of NFTs.

Once you have created your NFTs, they will be stored on-chain and can no longer be modified. If you wish, you can put your NFTs up for sale. Featured by Binance currently supports two methods of selling within its secondary market: fixed price and auction (English style) sales.

As soon as the sales are completed, your NFTs will be distributed to buyers. Proceeds from sales will be transferred from the buyers' wallets to yours. This process is automated and protected by various rules defined in smart contracts.

NFT Marketplace (Custodial)

To sell your NFT on a custodial marketplace, you will need to deposit it on the platform you wish to use. Make sure the platform accepts the type of NFT you want to sell. If you're not careful at this stage, you can easily lose your NFTs by sending them to an incompatible platform. Each marketplace will have different options for sale, such as fixed price or auction.

After you have successfully sold your NFT, the marketplace will automatically transfer it to the new owner. Your funds will be sent directly to your external wallet or left on the platform to be withdrawn.

Pros and cons of a custodial NFT service

A custodial NFT service is an easy way to bring buyers and sellers together, especially for those unfamiliar with this world. There is no worry of losing your keys, which is a relief for even the most experienced users. Interfaces are generally easy to use and the whole process is more flexible in case someone makes a mistake. In case a problem occurs, the platform should give you support.

On the other hand, for many crypto enthusiasts who value decentralization, not having direct control over their assets can be a major drawback. KYC checks are also required on some custodial NFT services, these require your name, address and proof of identity. Once this data is stored, there is always a risk of it being stolen or hacked. Some custodial services have been hacked in the past.

Pros and cons of a non-custodial NFT service

Non-custodial NFT platforms offer greater control throughout the transaction process. Trading NFT directly from your wallet without the presence of intermediaries provides cheaper transaction fees and greater privacy. However, these factors are highly dependent on the network you are using. If privacy is important to you, in this case it is not necessary to carry out KYC checks, so you can operate anonymously. All you need is a wallet to get started.

There are some downsides to non-custodial wallets too. New users who are not familiar with wallets may have some difficulty with non-custodial options, which are less easy and convenient to use than custodial ones. Fortunately, some service providers like Tor.us are making it easier to use.

As of June 2021, non-custodial exchanges tend to have lower liquidity and volumes than custodial ones, with the exception of large players such as Uniswap. However, when it comes to NFTs, the industry is still in its infancy, which makes it difficult to measure accurately. Liquidity depends substantially on two factors: the user base and the trading volume; there is a good chance that non-custodial services will overtake custodial services in the near future. There are also projects working on cross-platform non-custodial marketplaces, which are likely to solve liquidity problems.

A summary look at custodial vs non-custodial NFTs

Custodial NFT services – Non-custodial NFT services

Private Key - Third Party Property

Accessibility

Need for a registered account - Accessible to anyone

Transaction costs

Typically high - Typically low

Safety

Typically low - Typically high

Support

Typically high - Typically low

KYC

Yes - No

Depending on what you are looking for, the custodial and non-custodial options offer specific benefits. A non-custodial NFT platform like Featured By Binance is a great choice for anyone who values autonomy and security.

For inexperienced users, it may be easier to use an NFT marketplace and a custodial wallet. Custody services allow you to spend more time interacting on the platform and less time learning how to use wallets. In this case, Binance NFT Marketplace is a great option to consider.